AUSTRALIAN REGIONAL FOOD
The Best Chefs' Recipes

AUSTRALIAN REGIONAL FOOD
The Best Chefs' Recipes

Sally Hammond

First published in Australia in 2005 by

New Holland Publishers (Australia) Pty Ltd

Sydney · Auckland · London · Cape Town

14 Aquatic Drive Frenchs Forest New South Wales 2086 Australia

218 Lake Road Northcote Auckland New Zealand

86 Edgware Road London W2 2EA United Kingdom

80 McKenzie Street Cape Town 8001 South Africa

A record of this book is available from the National Library of Australia.

ISBN: 1 74110 394 0

Publisher: Fiona Schultz

Project Editor: Lliane Clarke

Designer: Greg Lamont

Production Manager: Grace Gutwein

Printer: C&C Offset

10 9 8 7 6 5 4 3 2 1

Cover photographs:

Top left: Ashbolts Farm, Top right: Gordon Hammond, Bottom left: Gordon Hammond,

Back cover: Gordon Hammond.

Photos: Gordon Hammond, pages 11, 13, 14, 18, 20, 21, 23, 33, 55, 63, 64, 74, 80, 86, 107, 118, 121, 133, 135, 141, 143, 144, 159, 164. Henry Gosling. 15. Moorilla Estate, 17, 41, 42, 115, 131. Hunter Belle Cheese, 19. Gaia Retreat and Spa, 25. Alla Wolf-Tasker, 11, 34. Stillwater River Cafe, 44. Bellarine Estate, 47, 50. Sydney Seafood School, 56, 60. Alive Foods, 57. Neila Restaurant, 66. High Valley Wine & Cheese, 71. Spirit House, 81. Penfolds Magill Estate, 82, 83. Dennis Klump, 85. Ashbolts Farm, 89. Les Goldsmith, 102. Voyager Estate, 103, 109. Simply Green Tomatoes, 111. Fee and Me, 138, 139. Duck Under the Table, 147. Borrodell on the Mount, 152. Proven Artisan Breads and Pastries, 153.

ACKNOWLEDGMENTS

I would like to thank all those busy people who took the time after a long day of running a restaurant, or pressing, bottling, baking, picking or milking, or perhaps in the midst of making cheese or chutney, bread or sausages, to put together a few of their best recipes and share them generously with the rest of us.

All those who responded to our request, those who sent photographs, and those who patiently replied to our questions about the recipes or ingredients, deserve a round of applause.

Of course thanks are due to my patient editor at New Holland, Lliane Clarke, and to Fiona Schultz, New Holland's Publisher, for having the vision to commission this book.

And as always, my husband, Gordon, partner in work and life, has contributed immensely to this book, sorting through the photographs which were sent, fine-tuning them, and providing others from his huge file. Where would I be without him?

Sally Hammond
www.australianregionalfoodguide.com

Contents

Introduction... 10

    Substitutes and measurements............................ 11

Breakfast

Tasmania: The South 14

Queensland: Sunshine Coast 15

Entrees

New South Wales: Explorer Country and Riverina 18

New South Wales: Hunter Valley 19

New South Wales: North Coast 20

New South Wales: Northern Rivers 23

Queensland: Sunshine Coast 26

Victoria: Bays and Peninsulas 27

Victoria: Murray and the Outback............................ 30

Victoria: Yarra Valley and the Dandenong Ranges.............. 31

Victoria: Macedon Ranges and Spa Country 34

South Australia: Adelaide and Surrounds 36

South Australia: Kangaroo Island............................. 37

Western Australia: The South-West........................... 38

Western Australia: Perth and Surrounds 39

Tasmania: Hobart and Surrounds 40

Tasmania: The North 43

Salads

New South Wales: Explorer Country and Riverina 48

Victoria: Bays and Peninsulas 49

Victoria: Macedon Ranges and Spa Country 51

South Australia: Adelaide and Surrounds 52

Western Australia: Australia's North-West 53

Soups

New South Wales: Sydney and The Southern Highlands 56

Queensland: Sunshine Coast 57

Victoria: Legends, Wine and High Country 58

South Australia: Clare Valley and Yorke Peninsula 59

Mains

New South Wales: Explorer Country and Riverina 64

New South Wales: Hunter Valley 67

New South Wales: Explorer Country and Riverina 71

New South Wales: North Coast 72

New South Wales: Northern Rivers 75

New South Wales: South Coast and Illawarra 76

Queensland: Far North 77

Queensland: Bundaberg, Fraser Coast and Sth Burnett 80

Queensland: Sunshine Coast 81

South Australia: Adelaide and Surrounds 82

South Australia: Barossa 84

Tasmania: Bass Strait Islands 85

Tasmania: The North 86

Victoria: Bays and Peninsulas 94

Victoria: Legends, Wine and High Country 96

Victoria: Lakes and Wilderness. 102

Victoria: Murray and the Outback 104

Victoria: Macedon Ranges and Spa Country. 106

Western Australia: The South-West 108

Accompaniments

New South Wales: Hunter Valley 112

Victoria: Murray and the Outback. 112

Desserts

New South Wales: Blue Mountains and The Hawkesbury 116

New South Wales: Hunter Valley 117

New South Wales: North Coast. 118

New South Wales: Northern Rivers 124

Queensland: Sunshine Coast 125

South Australia: Adelaide and Surrounds. 126

South Australia: Barossa 130

Tasmania: Hobart and Surrounds 132

Tasmania: The North 135

Tasmania: The North-West. 140

Victoria: Murray and The Outback 142

Victoria: Yarra Valley and the Dandenong Ranges 142

Western Australia: Australia's North-West 145

Biscuits

New South Wales: North Coast 148

South Australia: Adelaide and Surrounds. 148

South Australia: Barossa 149

Cakes and breads

New South Wales: Explorer Country and Riverina 152

Victoria: Legends, Wine and High Country 154

Victoria: Goldfields. 155

Victoria: Yarra Valley and the Dandenong Ranges 156

Western Australia: The South-West 157

South Australia: Adelaide Hills. 157

Jams, relishes and spreads

New South Wales: Hunter Valley. 160

Queensland: Sunshine Coast 160

South Australia: Clare Valley and Yorke Peninsula 161

Western Australia: Australia's Coral Coast. 163

Drinks

New South Wales: Explorer Country and Riverina 165

Victoria: Legends, Wine and High Country 165

Australian Regional Producers and Chefs 166

Australian Regional Maps. 169

INDEX 173

Introduction

When Gordon and I put together the *Australian Regional Food Guide* with New Holland in 2004 we were amazed at the wealth of talent, energy and entrepreneurial spirit throughout this country.

It was but a short step to decide that some of these people might like to share some of their recipes, hints, tips and culinary knowledge. When we asked them, we were delighted with the response. Here we have recipes from everywhere—from some of the top chefs in the land to individuals and small companies producing unusual foods. All of these recipes have been tested by the people who sent them. We asked each of them, 'how often do you make this?' and many said, 'every week' or, 'it's always on our menu'.

These recipes do not look the way they arrived on my desk. They have been styled to suit home cooking in the belief that most Australian cooks use cups and tablespoons rather than scales—measures rather than weights—although in some cases weights have been included in brackets. The main aim is for clarity and ease of use.

REGIONAL PRODUCTS AND THEIR SUBSTITUTES

The recipes come from all over regional Australia and some call for a branded product associated with the person supplying the recipe. You can contact the chef or the restaurant for details of stockists. We have listed these at the back of the book. Many places have mail order and online ordering. Of course you can always substitute a similar ingredient or product.

Some recipes include wine suggestions, usually when the recipe has come from a winery. It seemed only right they should suggest one of their own wines. Try their suggestion, or substitute a similar wine.

Likewise, many cheese-makers develop recipes to suit their own cheeses, and we strongly suggest you try to find that particular cheese for the best result with the dish. (Contact the cheese-maker for

stockists near you.) Of course, feel free to substitute the same variety of cheese from another source if it is unavailable. Just be aware the results may differ.

Many of the contributors decided to add their own notes and hints to make the dish 'their way' and their advice is invaluable—a little like a peek into Grandma's handwritten cookery books.

The most important thing is that these recipes will not only make your mouth water, but they will send you scurrying to the kitchen to try them for yourself. And as you enjoy them with your family and friends you will rejoice in the culinary richness and talent of this vast country.

A NOTE ABOUT MEASUREMENTS

Everyone measures things differently. For consistency throughout the book, these recipes have been adapted to the accepted style of most Australian cookbooks.

Rather than using metric weights, the quantities of most loose and dry ingredients have been expressed in cups and tablespoons. The quantities for cheese, fats (unless melted), meat, fruit, vegetables and some packaged goods, are usually given in kilograms and grams (kg, g), in the belief that these will have been bought by weight and perhaps still be marked with the weight. In this case, it is often easier to calculate the amount and then take the appropriate portion.

Liquids are expressed as litres and mls, as most kitchens use a measuring jug marked in this way, but for smaller amounts, tablespoons are used.

For reference, the Australian metric tablespoon is 20ml, a teaspoon 5ml, a cup 250ml, or 4 cups to the litre. If using a jug, recalculate the amount. Many dry amounts correspond—250g is a cup (usually), but flour for instance measures 125g to the cup. Cup–weight equivalents get tricky when you try to convert such ingredients as coconut, oatmeal, crushed nuts, sultanas or beans, so some recipes in this book may still give the weight.

Breakfast

This recipe was developed for Sorell Fruit Farm by Judith Sweet, a leading Tasmanian food writer and food critic. These delicious treats are also ideal as dessert. Don't worry about consuming wine so early in the morning, as the alcohol evaporates with the cooking.

HOTCAKES with CHERRY LIQUEUR SAUCE   Serves 4

1½ cups self raising flour
½ teaspoon salt
½ teaspoon ground cinnamon
2 tablespoons sugar
2 eggs
1¼ cups milk
2 tablespoons vegetable oil

Combine flour, salt, cinnamon and sugar thoroughly. Beat eggs and milk together and mix into the flour mixture. Stir until blended then beat in the oil, and let stand for half an hour to an hour. For each hotcake pour approximately a quarter cup of mixture onto a lightly greased pan over moderate heat. Cook until bubbles appear on the surface then turn and cook the other side. Serve while still hot with Cherry Liqueur Sauce.

CHERRY LIQUEUR SAUCE

1 cup pitted sour cherries, drained
200ml juice from the jar
2 tablespoons brown sugar
5–6cm stick of cinnamon
100ml Thornlea Wines
Cherry Liqueur

This sauce contains no thickeners so that it can soak in and flavour the hotcakes. Prepare the sauce while the hotcake mixture is standing. Sour cherries, sold in a jar, are used for this sauce. Put all the ingredients together in a small saucepan and bring to the boil. Simmer until the juices are reduced by a third. Remove the cinnamon stick and serve hot over the hotcakes

Elaine and Bob Hardy, Sorell Fruit Farm, Sorell

'This Kenilworth ricotta breakfast recipe was created because we are vegetarians,' says Henry Gosling.

KENILWORTH RICOTTA BREAKFAST　　　　Serves 4

200g Kenilworth ricotta,
sliced 1cm thick
4 medium tomatoes, halved
1 bunch spinach or silver beet,
chopped roughly
salt and pepper to taste
fresh basil, chopped

Brown ricotta slices under a grill, then grill tomatoes. Steam spinach or silver beet with a small amount of water in a saucepan. Top drained spinach or silver beet with two slices of grilled ricotta and grilled tomatoes. Season to taste and garnish with basil.

Henry Gosling, Kenilworth Country Foods, Kenilworth

Entrees

'This recipe was taught to me by my mother when I was ten years old,' says Bechora Deeb (left). 'It has been adjusted to local and seasonal products.' These include fresh vine leaves, tomatoes, oil, mint and parsley, and lemons.

STUFFED VINE LEAVES
Serves 6–8

2 cups rice (Calrose short grain), uncooked
1 bunch continental (flat leaf) parsley
1 bunch mint
1 bunch spring onions
4 medium tomatoes
½ cup pine nuts, toasted
salt and black pepper
70 fresh vine leaves
1 cup olive oil
1 cup lemon juice

Soak rice in hot water for 20 minutes. Meanwhile finely chop herbs, onions and tomatoes. Drain rice and add all chopped ingredients plus pine nuts, and salt and pepper to taste.

Arrange 50 of the best vine leaves face down on a bench, placing a heaped teaspoon of the rice mixture on each leaf. Roll up from stalk end, tucking in the ends. Place 20 coarser vine leaves in the bottom of a medium saucepan, then place the rolled vine leaves on top, ensuring that they are firmly wedged into position and not liable to move during cooking. Cover gently with warm water and oil.

Place an upturned plate on top of the vine leaves. Put saucepan lid on and simmer gently for 15–20 minutes. Add lemon juice and simmer for a further 5 minutes. Turn off heat, cool and refrigerate overnight.

Before serving, remove plate and, holding the lid on firmly, turn upside-down to allow the juice to roll through the leaves gently. Carefully remove from saucepan and serve.

Bechora Deeb, Deeb's Kitchen, Mudgee

'This is just like a restaurant meal at home and was a hit with the family in the Hunter Belle Cheese test kitchen,' says Kate Woodward (below). 'It even got my boys eating greens!'

CHAR-GRILLED BEEF or LAMB
& GOLDENBELLE STACK ON MESCLUN   Serves 5

1½ tablespoons balsamic vinegar
1½ tablespoons olive oil
½ tablespoon honey
½ garlic clove, crushed
freshly ground black pepper, to taste
125g mesclun (salad mix)
50g raisins
150g bacon rashers, cut into fine strips, fried until crisp
750g beef or lamb fillets
250g thinly sliced Goldenbelle washed rind cheese
50g toasted pine nuts

Whisk together vinegar, oil, honey, garlic and pepper to form a dressing. Combine mesclun, raisins and bacon. For each serving char-grill a 150g beef or lamb fillet until well-sealed and done to your liking. Rest five minutes before slicing diagonally. Toss dressing through a portion of mesclun salad (approx. 1½ cups each) and arrange on serving plates. Stack slices of fillet on top of each salad and top with two slices of Goldenbelle cheese and a sprinkle of pine nuts.

Kate Woodward, Hunter Belle Cheese, Muswellbrook

'To create new dishes is like introducing new actors into the play —we tried to keep it tasty and simple,' says Wolfgang Zichy (right, with Catherine McDonald). 'So when Barrington perch (silver perch) was on offer, we came up with a different idea to serve it.' The perch is farmed in pristine waters in Gloucester, close to the Barrington Tops.

BARRINGTON PERCH FILLETS POACHED in a LEMON MYRTLE MACADAMIA NUT COCONUT SAUCE
Serves 4

2½ tablespoons good olive oil

2 brown onions, finely chopped

3 garlic cloves, crushed

2 kaffir lime leaves

1½ teaspoons ground lemon myrtle

2 teaspoons lemongrass, finely chopped

2 small tins of coconut cream

4 Barrington perch (silver perch), skinless

2 tablespoons shallots, finely chopped

2 tablespoons leek, finely chopped

4 portions of steamed Arborio rice

½ bunch of coriander, finely chopped

120g macadamia nuts, chopped

Heat oil in a large pan, add onions and garlic and saute without colouring. Add kaffir lime leaves, lemon myrtle and lemongrass. Stir gently, add coconut cream and bring almost to the boil. Add fish, making sure pieces are submerged and simmer for five minutes or until fish is cooked through. Add shallots and leeks and simmer for one minute.

Place steamed Arborio rice on four plates, flatten slightly. Place perch fillets on top of the rice, divide coconut cream stock and ladle over the fish. Serve sprinkled with chopped coriander and macadamias.

Wolfgang Zichy, The Moorings Restaurant and Cafe, Harrington

Moorings recommends serving Tallawanta 2003 Semillon Sauvignon Blanc with this dish.

GRAVLAX & CAVIAR in BUTTERMILK JELLY

Serves 6

½ teaspoon ground coriander
½ teaspoon freshly ground pepper
2 teaspoons sugar
1 ¼ tablespoons salt
400g salmon fillets, with skin on
1 bunch basil, chopped
2 lemons, sliced

Mix coriander, pepper, sugar and salt and rub it into the salmon.

Place salmon on cling wrap (skin side down), then top with chopped basil and lemon slices. Wrap salmon in cling wrap and refrigerate for 24 hours.

BUTTERMILK JELLY

750ml buttermilk
pinch salt and pepper to taste
juice of half a lemon
2 tablespoons Noilly Prat (or a high quality vermouth)
100ml fish stock, warmed
12 leaves of gelatin, softened
200ml cream, whipped
100g caviar
extra caviar
basil to garnish

For the jelly, mix buttermilk, salt, pepper, lemon juice and Noilly Prat. Fold fish stock and gelatin into the buttermilk mixture and when it starts to set, fold in whipped cream. Remove spice and herb marinade from salmon with kitchen paper, take the skin off and slice into thin slices.

Assemble jelly, salmon and caviar in layers in a terrine form and refrigerate up to 6 hours. To serve, dip terrine form into hot water and tip terrine onto a cutting board. Dip knife into hot water, slice jelly into 2cm thick slices, and place on plates.

Top with extra caviar and serve, topped with fresh basil.

Wolfgang Zichy , The Moorings Restaurant and Cafe, Harrington

SAUTEED PRAWNS & SCALLOPS
with LEMON MYRTLE

Serves 4

1 tablespoon olive oil
2 tablespoons finely chopped spring
onions
12 medium green king prawns,
peeled and deveined
8 scallops, trimmed
salt and cracked black pepper
(or Dorrigo pepper)
ground dried lemon myrtle to taste
(between 1 teaspoon and
1 dessertspoon)
½ cup semillon
cooked rice

Heat the oil and cook onions until translucent—around a minute will do. Increase heat and add the prawns and scallops. Add salt and pepper to taste. Cook for a minute or until the prawns are firm to the touch and sprinkle on lemon myrtle. Pour in the wine and cook to reduce a little. This whole process will take 4-5 minutes. Serve with cooked rice.

Barbara Barlin, Barbushco Pty Ltd, Lorne

FISH CAKES with MANGO & LEMON MYRTLE DRESSING

Serves 4

425g can tuna, drained and flaked
1 onion, finely diced
2 potatoes, boiled and mashed
1 carrot, grated
1 egg, beaten
½ cup breadcrumbs
(or use Barbushco Bush Dukkah)
2 tablespoons Barbushco Mango &
Lemon Myrtle Dressing

Mix all ingredients thoroughly. Divide into tablespoon portions and shape into patties. Coat with additional breadcrumbs and fry in a little oil or butter 5–7 minutes each side.

Barbara Barlin, Barbushco, Lorne

These oysters are simple and quick to prepare and are a big hit at parties. When chef Steven Snow makes them for his award-winning restaurant, he uses Wallis Lake oysters and kaffir lime leaves from his own garden in Possum Creek.

STEAMED SYDNEY ROCK OYSTERS with KAFFIR LIME, CHILLI, GINGER & TAMARI

Serves 2

12 Sydney rock or Pacific oysters in the shell, freshly shucked
1 kaffir lime leaf, cut lengthwise in 1mm shreds
2cm piece fresh ginger, peeled and cut in julienne
1 red banana chilli, seeded and finely sliced
1¼ tablespoons tamari or light soy sauce
squeeze of lime juice

Place oysters in a 25cm bamboo steamer basket and top each with pieces of kaffir lime leaf, ginger and chilli. Add water to the depth of 1 centimetre in a wok and bring to the boil. Place steamer basket over wok, cover with a lid and steam for 1 minute 45 seconds. Do not overcook. Serve oysters in steamer basket or place on a plate, drizzle with tamari and an optional squeeze of lime juice, and serve immediately.

Steven Snow, Fins Seafood Restaurant,
Waterfront Beach Hotel, Byron Bay

CRISPY WONTON PRAWNS with
RED PAWPAW SALSA, LIME & TOMATO CHUTNEY   Serves 4

16 medium to large green prawns
½ teaspoon sea salt
8 square wonton wrappers, cut in half diagonally
1 teaspoon cornflour, dissolved in 2 teaspoons cold water

Remove prawn heads and shells, leaving on the tail section. De-vein by running a knife down the back of each prawn and removing the vein. Sprinkle prawns with sea salt.

Place the head-end of each prawn in the base of each wonton triangle and dab each base corner with the cornflour and water mixture. Fold over and stick together. Once done, store covered and refrigerated until ready to cook.

SALSA

1 red pawpaw, peeled, deseeded and cut into 3cm cubes
2 kaffir lime leaves, central stem removed and thinly sliced
1 garlic clove, finely chopped
1¼ tablespoons sweet chilli sauce
mizuna or mixed young leaves
4 sprigs fresh coriander
500ml vegetable oil for frying

Make a salsa by mixing pawpaw, kaffir lime leaves, garlic and sweet chilli sauce. Let this salsa sit chilled for about 30 minutes for flavours to infuse. Wash and dry mizuna and pick leaflets off coriander. In centre of each plate place some mizuna or young leaves with some coriander leaves. Place approximately three dessertspoons of pawpaw salsa on top of leaves.

Heat oil in a pot to 180°C. Drop wrapped prawns in six at a time, and cook until wonton wrappers are golden and crisp, approximately 2 minutes. Remove prawns and drain on paper towels. Place four prawns standing around the salsa and, with a teaspoon, dab a little lime and tomato chutney (recipe follows) on each one. Serve immediately.

LIME & TOMATO CHUTNEY

2 tablespoons lime pickle
1 handful pitted dates
1 cup diced tinned tomatoes
pinch salt
1 birdseye chilli, deseeded and chopped (optional)
¼ cup water

Place all ingredients together in pot and cook on low heat, stirring occasionally for 15 minutes. Dates should be softened and the mix should still be quite thick. Blend all ingredients in a food processor until smooth and set aside in bowl.

Todd Cameron, Gaia Retreat and Spa, Bangalow

All the preparation for this dish can be done well beforehand. It's in three parts, yet each part is very simple with no hard-to-get ingredients. 'It is the favourite dish of our guests,' says Todd Cameron. 'The crispy wonton wrapper around the prawns is the perfect contrast to the sweet, delicious pawpaw with spicy, tangy chutney. Don't try this with yellow pawpaw as it is never as good.'

This is ideal as a snack or as AN entree when having friends around for dinner.

KENILWORTH BRUSCHETTA   Serves 4

2 medium tomatoes, chopped into small cubes
2 finely chopped fresh basil leaves
2 garlic cloves, crushed
100g Kenilworth feta, mashed
salt
freshly ground black pepper
4 long slices French bread, cut diagonally
2 tablespoons olive oil
garlic salt

Combine tomato, basil, garlic and feta in a bowl and season to taste with salt and pepper. Allow mixture to stand for 20 minutes to blend flavours. Brush French bread with oil and sprinkle lightly with garlic salt. Heat under the grill and lightly toast on both sides. Top each slice of toasted French bread with the tomato and feta mixture. Serve immediately or heat under the grill as liked.

Henry Gosling, Kenilworth Country Foods, Kenilworth

Pettavel Winery's Chef Richard Hooper uses buffalo mozzarella from Shaw River, which is near Portland, for this recipe.

BUFFALO MOZZARELLA with EGGPLANT CAPONATA

Serves 4

½ small eggplant, diced into 8mm cubes
olive oil to saute
2 stalks celery, diced into 8mm cubes
1 tablespoon lilliput capers
1 tablespoon finely chopped parsley
1 tablespoon very finely chopped lemon zest
additional olive oil
salt and pepper to taste
200g buffalo mozzarella, cut into thick wedges
salt flakes

Saute the eggplant in a very hot fry pan in a little olive oil. Aim to achieve a golden colour on all sides of the eggplant cubes. Remove from the heat and reserve the eggplant in a bowl.

Repeat this step for the celery, taking care not to overcook. It should retain a nice crunch when you bite into it. Mix the eggplant, celery, capers, parsley, lemon zest and a little olive oil in a bowl. Taste and add salt and pepper.

Arrange this mixture, called a caponata, in the middle of a plate and place the wedges of mozzarella on top. Sprinkle with some salt flakes and finish with a drizzle of olive oil.

Richard Hooper, Pettavel Winery and Restaurant, Waurn Ponds

Ideally accompanied by a glass of Pettavel 2002 Pinot Noir.

Pettavel Winery's Chef Richard Hooper grows artichokes in his kitchen garden, five metres from the back door, for this recipe. They are also grown locally in Ceres, a hamlet about five minutes away.

ARTICHOKES FROM THE GARDEN
with BASQUE FLAVOURED SALSA

Serves 4 as tapas

8 small firm artichokes
4 lemons, cut in halves
2 litres water
150ml seeded mustard dressing

Peel and cut off the outer leaves from the artichokes, then rub the ends with lemon. Put the artichokes and lemons together in a pot of water and weigh down with a plate so that the artichokes cook under the surface of the water. The artichokes will take about 6 to 7 minutes to cook after the water has come to the boil. Test the artichokes by pushing the tip of a paring knife into the base. If the knife pushes in easily, the artichoke is cooked.

Remove artichokes from the water and place in a colander to drain well. Coat thoroughly with two-thirds of the seeded mustard dressing.

BASQUE FLAVOURED SALSA

2 garlic cloves, diced very finely
¼ green capsicum, diced very finely
2 French shallots, diced very finely
¼ red capsicum, diced very finely
4 cornichons, diced very finely
1 tablespoon parsley
very finely chopped
salt and pepper to taste

Combine diced ingredients and parsley in a bowl, and mix with the remaining third of the seeded mustard dressing as a salsa. Season to taste with salt and pepper. Halve artichokes and arrange attractively on a platter. Using a teaspoon, garnish the artichokes with a neat scoop of the salsa.

Richard Hooper, Pettavel Winery and Restaurant, Waurn Ponds

Enjoy with a glass of Pettavel Sauvignon Blanc Semillon.

BEETROOT & FETA RISOTTO   Serves 6

4 medium beetroot
1.7 litres vegetable stock
1½ tablespoons olive oil
100g finely diced shallots
4 garlic cloves, crushed
400g supa-fino Arborio rice
100g feta, cut in 1cm dice
150g butter, diced
80g Parmesan cheese, grated as finely as possible
salt and pepper

Enjoy with a Pettavel 2003 Platina Merlot Petit Verdot.

Roast the beetroot with the skin still on until tender, allow to cool and then peel and dice into 1cm cubes. Bring vegetable stock to the boil and add half the beetroot, allowing to simmer for 20 minutes, then strain and discard the beetroot, or put aside to use in another dish. Bring the now beetroot-flavoured vegetable stock back to the boil.

In a heavy-bottomed saucepan heat the olive oil then add shallots and garlic and saute, stirring with a wooden spoon for 30 seconds before adding rice. Keep the rice moving gently, ladle in 200ml of the stock and keep stirring the rice. Adjust the temperature of the rice to a medium heat while keeping the stock boiling.

Add the stock one ladleful at a time, making sure all of the previous stock is absorbed before adding the next ladleful. Keep tasting the rice to get to the degree of doneness you like. When satisfied, add the remaining diced beetroot, butter, feta and Parmesan and fold together. Check the flavour, adding salt and pepper to taste, then allow the risotto to sit for 2 minutes.

Richard Hooper, Pettavel Winery and Restaurant, Waurn Ponds

Marilyn Lanyon has been making Simply Green Tomatoes, a unique green tomato product, for many years, and now prepares it in a commercial kitchen on her tomato-growing property located approximately 15 minutes from Boort, not far from the Murray River. This is described by Marilyn as a simple pre-dinner nibble or entrée.

SIMPLE NIBBLE MUSHROOMS

Makes 10

10 medium-sized field mushrooms, wiped clean, stems removed
10 slices of Simply Green Tomatoes
1 tablespoon feta or tasty cheese
1 tablespoon breadcrumbs

Place one slice of Simply Green Tomatoes in the cavity of each mushroom. Crumble a little cheese over each tomato slice and sprinkle the tops with breadcrumbs. Place the mushrooms on a tray and grill slowly until the mushrooms are a little tender and the topping is lightly browned.

SIMPLY GREEN DIP OR SPREAD

Makes 1 cups

2 tablespoons Simply Green Tomatoes, chopped finely
The reserved extra virgin olive oil can be used for pan frying chicken, fish, or steak, or in salad dressings.
1 cup light cream cheese

Blend both ingredients together until smooth. Use as a dip, fill a piping bag and pipe small amounts onto crackers, or use as a spread on sandwiches.

Marilyn Lanyon, Simply Tomatoes, Boort

'This is a modern and lighter adaptation of the French classic pork rillettes,' says John Knoll. 'I wanted a lighter dish that customers could graze on. Many choose to spread it on local toasted Fruition sourdough. It's the perfect starter.'

YARRA VALLEY SALMON RILLETTES
with PICKLED FENNEL SALAD
Serves 8

500g Yarra Valley salmon fillet
sea salt
white pepper
150g unsalted butter, softened
1 teaspoon lemon zest
juice 1 lemon
½ cup homemade mayonnaise
2 tablespoons finely chopped capers
1 tablespoon finely chopped chives

Season salmon fillet with salt and pepper and steam for 7 minutes or until just cooked. Shred salmon with two forks. Allow to cool. Cream butter, fold in salmon and remaining ingredients gently, and spoon into individual ramekins. Accompany with Pickled Fennel Salad (recipe below), fresh toasted sourdough and rocket.

PICKLED FENNEL SALAD

1 bulb fennel, thinly sliced
¼ cup table salt
½ Spanish onion, thinly sliced
1½ cups white wine vinegar
1 cup white sugar
1 teaspoon mustard seeds
½ teaspoon celery seeds
½ teaspoon green peppercorns

Cover fennel with cold water, add salt, and refrigerate overnight. Drain and rinse. Combine remaining ingredients and simmer for 5 minutes. Add fennel to hot pickling mix and simmer for 5 minutes until fennel is tender. Seal and store, refrigerated, until needed.

John Knoll, Mt Rael Retreat, Healesville

'Being Scottish, I like smoked fish,' says Gordon Brown. 'I have married this delicate, moist method of cooking with the subtlety of mascarpone and the strength of capers to match the smoky flavours of the fish. The recipe was originally used at a regional wine and food event requiring light food that was easy to serve and which highlighted regional produce.'

BLACK PADDOCK TERRINE OF SALMON with CAPERS & MASCARPONE

Serves 10, depending on thickness of slices

1 side of Thornton Farm salmon, skinned and pin-boned
4 sheets gelatin
100ml fish stock
750g mascarpone
100g tiny capers
1 red capsicum, roasted and skinned, cut in julienne
bunch chives
250ml thickened cream
bunch fresh asparagus spears blanched.

Using a smoking oven, set up the tray with 1kg hickory chips, 2 crushed star anise, 250mm length chardonnay vine (cut up into small pieces), 30g tea leaves and 2 cinnamon sticks. Smoke the salmon until pink in texture and a light golden brown in colour for 8–10 minutes. Remove from the heat, flake, and set aside to cool.

In a small pan, dissolve gelatin sheets in the fish stock. Set aside without allowing it to cool. In a metal bowl, combine mascarpone, tiny capers, red capsicum and chives, then add the flaked salmon and thickened cream. Line a terrine mould with cling wrap and set aside. Add the gelatin and fish stock liquor to the mascarpone and salmon mix and combine, seasoning to taste.

This is excellent accompanied with Evelyn County Estate Black Paddock Sauvignon Blanc or 2002 Chardonnay.

Using a spatula, layer the smoked salmon mix and asparagus in alternate layers, cover with cling wrap and allow to set in the fridge for 12 hours.

Serve with crusty bread and pickled cornichons.

Gordon Brown,
Evelyn County Estate's Black Paddock Restaurant,
Kangaroo Ground

TIPS FOR SMOKING

A homemade smoking oven can be easily assembled using two heavy-based oven trays (7–8cm high), a cake cooking rack and aluminium foil.

- Half-fill the bottom tray with hickory shavings, star anise, old chardonnary vine clippings, tea leaves, or cinnamon sticks. Run an edge of foil around the perimeter of the tray to ensure a good seal when the top tray is added. Place the oiled cooking rack over the hickory, place the fish on the rack and cover with the second tray to seal.
- Use a gas burner to conduct the heat, such as a barbecue, and cook for 10–15 minutes once the tray is smoking, depending on the thickness of the fillet, and degree of heat.
- Chicken and other meats can be smoked with equally delicious and succulent outcomes. Whatever the choice, take care not to overcook red meats beyond pink texture to optimise moist texture and tenderness and avoid the bitter after-taste that can result from smoking to dryness. Chicken, however, should be fully cooked.

PLEASE NOTE: Caution needs to be taken as the shavings can catch fire if left unattended.

'This dish is reminiscent of the smoked fish and blini combination so much a part of special occasion eating of my Russian childhood. The pancakes however are less of a chore to make than traditional blini.'

SALAD OF SMOKED EEL & SMOKED TROUT SAUSAGE on a POTATO PANCAKE
Serves 4

6 tablespoons olive oil

2 tablespoons red wine vinegar

a generous handful of seasonal baby salad greens

4 pieces smoked eel fillet, each about 5cm square, boned and skinned

8–12 diagonal slices of smoked trout sausage, lightly grilled (recipe below)

4 very thin bacon slices, fried crisp

1 tablespoon freshly grated horseradish

3 tablespoons whipped cream

Make a dressing from the olive oil and vinegar. Toss salad leaves in dressing and layer with a piece of smoked eel, 2-3 slices of Smoked Trout Sausage (recipe follows) and bacon on each of four warmed Potato Pancakes (recipe follows). Drizzle remaining dressing over and around each salad. Mix together horseradish and whipped cream and shape quenelles, placing one on top of each salad. Serve immediately.

SMOKED TROUT SAUSAGE

300g salmon, cleaned, boned, trimmed and chopped
1 egg white
200ml thickened cream
1 smoked trout, skinned, boned and diced
1 tablespoon chopped chives
salt and pepper
aluminium foil, cut in 15cm squares

Make sure that fish, egg white and cream are well chilled. Working quickly, process salmon to a fine puree in a processor. Add egg white and blend until well combined. Add half the quantity of cream, pulsing in gradually. Place mixture in a stainless steel bowl. Fold in smoked trout. Place in refrigerator for half an hour.

Remove from refrigerator, fold in the rest of the well-chilled cream. Add chopped chives and season with salt and pepper. Refrigerate. Place two tablespoons of mixture onto each foil square. Roll into sausage shape and twist both ends tight to finish sausages neatly. Refrigerate for at least an hour. Simmer the sausages gently in water for 1-2 minutes. If not using immediately, lay out on a tray to cool. Refrigerate. Remove sausages from foil and grill to serve or coat in butter and heat in oven.

Makes 10

POTATO PANCAKES

150g dry mashed potato
1 egg
1 tablespoon self raising flour
70ml milk, warmed
salt and pepper to taste
1 egg white
oil, for frying

Warm potato. Beat egg into potato until there are no lumps. Fold in sifted flour. Whisk in warm milk and season to taste. Whisk egg white until stiff and fold through potato mix. Gently pan fry tablespoons of the mixture, spreading into circles approximately 7cm in diameter. Turn over halfway through cooking time and ensure both sides are golden coloured. Remove from heat and cool on absorbent kitchen paper.

When cooled, trim with a 7cm diameter cutter. Reheat pancakes on oven tray at 160°C for 10 minutes.

Makes fifteen 7cm pancakes

Alla Wolf-Tasker, Lake House, Daylesford

BAKED CAPSICUM with GOAT CHEESE   Serves 4

4 large capsicums
4 truss or vine ripened tomatoes, quartered
2-3 cloves garlic, cut in slivers
4 anchovy fillets, chopped
fresh thyme, chopped
freshly ground salt and pepper
Talinga Grove extra virgin olive oil
$\frac{1}{2}$ cup fresh goat cheese (a crumbly variety) or goat curd

Slice capsicums in half and remove seeds and membranes. Pack tomatoes firmly into the capsicum. Dot with slivers of garlic (be generous) and chopped anchovy fillets (as much or as little as you wish). Sprinkle with fresh thyme leaves, season with salt and pepper and drizzle with a generous amount of olive oil. Pack into an ovenproof dish and bake in a moderate oven 30 minutes or until soft and slightly collapsed.

Remove from oven, top with crumbled goat cheese and return to oven for 5 minutes to warm the cheese. Serve with another drizzle of olive oil and a good chunk of woodfired oven bread to mop up all the juices.

This entree can be served immediately and tastes great, but 24 hours' marinating will intensify all the flavours.

HONEY GLAZED EGGPLANT TALINGA GROVE   Serves 4

2 small eggplants, cut into 3mm slices
salt and pepper
100ml Talinga Grove extra virgin olive oil
3 tablespoons white wine vinegar
4 tablespoons water
2 tablespoons honey
8 basil leaves, chopped
2 sprigs tarragon, chopped
$\frac{1}{4}$ bunch coriander

Season eggplant slices with salt and pepper and pan fry in olive oil until lightly golden. Separately, bring vinegar and water to the boil, remove, add honey and allow to stand. Place eggplant in a shallow dish, pour over honey and vinegar mix and allow to cool slightly. Sprinkle with herbs, cover with cling wrap, refrigerate and marinate for 24 hours.

Helen Morgan, Talinga Grove, Strathalbyn

This dish showcases local brie-style Borda White, a small, square soft-mould cheese, and locally gathered native wild cranberries. It's 'a firm fixture on the cafe menu' says Marion Chambers who developed it as 'a healthy alternative to crumbed and deep-fried camembert'. The coated cheese can also be stored, airtight in the fridge, for up to a week before cooking.

HAZELNUT BAKED BORDA WHITE   Serves 4

1 Borda White cheese
top thinly sliced off
1 egg, beaten with 1 teaspoon milk
or cream
¼ cup dried breadcrumbs
¼ cup ground hazelnuts
apples, crackers, cranberries to serve

Dip the top and sides of the cheese in the egg mixture. Mix breadcrumbs and hazelnuts, then dip the cheese in this. Place the cheese on a small square of baking paper on a tray and bake in a preheated 180°C oven for about 15 minutes, until golden.

Serve on a platter with sliced apples and crackers, accompanied by native Kangaroo Island cranberries or quince jelly.

Marion Chambers, Penguin Stop Cafe, Penneshaw

'This is one of our favourite dishes which I have taught at a cooking class we held here,' says Jill James. 'This pastry needs less work than one made with butter, as it mixes together very quickly—consequently it is very light and short. If eaten cold, I think it is better than pastry made wholly with a hard fat such as butter.'

BLACK OLIVE & THYME TART
with OLIVE OIL PASTRY

Serves 4

2 cups plain flour
pinch salt
4 tablespoons olive oil
200ml sour cream
4 eggs
300ml cream
100ml milk
3 tablespoons parmesan cheese
salt and pepper
150g black olives, roughly chopped (or 100g black olive tapenade)
1 onion, chopped
1 tablespoon olive oil
extra 100g black olives, roughly chopped
thyme leaves or sprigs
olive oil, extra

Place flour in the bowl of a food processor and add salt. Pour in olive oil and sour cream and briefly process until the mixture comes together. Don't overwork it. Rest the dough in the fridge for about 1 hour. Mix together eggs, cream, milk and parmesan, and season to taste. Put aside about 100ml, and stir olives or tapenade into the remainder. Saute onion in the oil. Line a greased tart pan with pastry, scatter sauteed onion over the base. Pour in the olive custard.

Cook for around 20 minutes in a preheated 180°C oven until the custard is just set but not fully cooked. Remove the tart from the oven and gently pour the reserved custard mix over the tart filling. Sprinkle over the extra black olives and some fresh thyme leaves or, for a more rustic look, some small sprigs of thyme.

Return tart to the oven and bake for approximately another 10 minutes. Drizzle the tart with a little olive oil when you remove it from the oven.

Jill James, Forest Grove Olive Oil Farm, Margaret River

This recipe was created by Kingsley and Chrissy Sullivan from New Norcia Bakery,' says Gabrielle Kervella. 'We've been good friends since they came to the West many years ago and started their wonderful sourdough breads made in wood-fired ovens.'

SMOKED SALMON with KERVELLA GOAT CHEESE in BREAD CASES

Makes 12 small appetisers

6 slices day old casalinga or rustic Italian bread, or French sourdough, cut thinly
soft butter
1 egg
2 tablespoons creme fraiche
salt and ground black pepper
1 large slice smoked salmon, cut into 12 pieces
70–80g fresh goat cheese, cut into 12 cubes
few sprigs of fresh thyme

Cut bread into rounds with a 6cm scone cutter. Spread soft butter onto one side of each round and place buttered side down into 12 mini muffin tins. Place a piece of smoked salmon and cube of goat cheese into each bread case. Whisk egg and creme fraiche together with salt and pepper (use sparingly) until combined. Pour a small amount of egg mixture into each bread case. Sprinkle with a few thyme leaves.

Bake for approximately 10 minutes in a preheated 200°C oven until eggs are set and cases are golden brown.

Gabrielle Kervella, Kervella Cheese , Gidgegannup

Macquarie Harbour ocean-run trout, Huon Valley Granny Smith apples, Spreyton avocados, and Houston's mizuna (Coal Valley) feature in this dish. Even the vine canes are sourced from the Estate.

HOT SMOKED OCEAN TROUT, APPLE & AVOCADO SALAD with LIMONCELLO DRESSING   Serves 4

100g rock salt
2 litres water, at room temperature
1 side ocean trout skin on, pin-boned
vine canes or wood chips for smoking
thinly sliced Granny Smith apple
thinly sliced avocado
mizuna leaves

Dissolve salt in water. Immerse trout in this brine for one hour. Dry well in a clean cloth. In a smoker or bain marie, heat woodchips over a medium heat until well smoking. Place fish on a wire rack and lower into the smoker.

Cover with foil and reduce heat to the lowest setting. Smoke for approximately 20 minutes until flesh is firm but still pink in the centre. The smoking time will depend on weight and thickness of the fillets. Remove and cool in fridge.

To serve, break up trout into bite-sized pieces. Thinly slice apple and avocado and layer with the trout and mizuna. Season to taste and drizzle with limoncello dressing.

LIMONCELLO DRESSING

1 cup water
600g castor sugar
1 cup (250ml) limoncello liqueur
2½ tablespoons white wine vinegar
pinch salt
2½ tablespoons extra virgin olive oil

Boil water and sugar to a light caramel. Add limoncello and vinegar and return to heat for one minute. Add salt and oil and cool to room temperature.

Justin Harris, Source Restaurant, Moorilla Estate, Berriedale

Best served chilled with a glass of 2004 Moorilla Estate White Label Riesling.

This recipe makes use of Connorville venison (Central Tasmania), Island Olive Groves extra virgin olive oil (Coal Valley) and hazelnuts from Tasmania's Channel region.

VENISON CARPACCIO with CHOCOLATE OIL & HAZELNUT CRUNCH

Serves 4

400g boned venison leg, trimmed

Roll venison leg in cling wrap and partially freeze. Slice into 1mm rounds and leave at room temperature. To serve, arrange venison slices flat across the serving plate. Drizzle with Chocolate Oil and scatter with Hazelnut Crunch (recipes follow). Accompany with a small salad of radicchio, rocket and cress.

HAZELNUT CRUNCH

500g castor sugar
100ml light soy sauce
100ml water
400g roasted hazelnuts

Bring sugar, soy sauce and water to boil in a pan until a light caramel is achieved. Be careful; do not use a shallow pan as this will have a tendency to rise. Stir in hazelnuts and pour onto greaseproof paper to cool. When set, crush lightly in a food processor. Store, airtight, at room temperature.

CHOCOLATE OIL

500ml extra virgin olive oil
300g grated Ibara chocolate
small pinch salt

Heat oil to 45°C. Remove from heat and whisk in chocolate. Add salt and strain through a fine chinois or sieve. Store at room temperature.

Justin Harris, Source Restaurant, Moorilla Estate, Berriedale

Best served with a full bodied Pinot Noir.

PORK RILLETTES   Serves 8-12

2kg diced pork meat, belly or shoulder, or half and half
salt and pepper to taste

This is a simple recipe—but it makes for a very elegant entrée.

Put pork in a pot and cover with water, allowing to simmer until meat becomes light gold. Strain and reserve the juice then put meat through a blender or food processor. Return the meat to the pot, add salt and pepper and reheat, stirring constantly. Adjust the seasoning to taste, remembering this needs plenty of salt and pepper.

While hot, transfer the rillettes to jars or a terrine. Let it cool down, then pour the juice over the meat and place jars in the fridge. It will be ready to eat after 48 hours.

Serve on toast with gherkins or cornichons.

Remi & Ginette Bancal , Peppers Calstock, Deloraine

TUNA TREVALLA SASHIMI   Serves 6-8

150g yellow fin tuna loin
170g trevalla/blue eye loin
2 cups fine egg noodles, cooked and cooled
150g baby spinach leaves, shredded
$\frac{1}{2}$ bunch coriander, chopped
1 punnet watercress sprouts, roughly chopped
freshly cracked black pepper
2 ruby grapefruit, skinned and segmented

Thinly slice both fish loins allowing 4–5 slices of each per person. Place noodles, shredded spinach, coriander, and half the watercress in a bowl. Sprinkle a little Roast Chilli Dressing (see below) over and mix ingredients well. Divide in equal portions on each serving plate, and crack a little pepper to taste over each.

Place fish in another bowl with remaining cress and grapefruit segments. Put a few teaspoons of dressing over as you are serving and gently fold through. Divide between each noodle stack. Add more dressing and serve immediately.

ROAST CHILLI DRESSING

1 chilli, roasted and ground
6 tablespoons light oil
6 tablespoons rice vinegar
6 tablespoons Kikkoman soy sauce
$\frac{1}{4}$ teaspoon wasabi powder
1 tablespoon grated red onion
4 tablespoons lime juice
a little cracked pepper

Grind the roasted chilli in a mortar and pestle. Combine with all other ingredients and chill until needed.

Don Cameron, Stillwater River Cafe, Launceston

Don Cameron devised this dish as a celebration of Tasmanian pinot noir and to showcase fabulous Tasmanian mushrooms and scallops. He suggests using a 'hot, hot pan' and briefly searing the scallops on each side so they don't dry out and become rubbery.

SEARED SCALLOPS with DOUBLE MUSHROOM CUSTARD, ROASTED BLACK MUSHROOMS & TOMATO BEURRE BLANC

Serves 6

300g butter, melted
2 stems each basil and parsley, finely chopped
6 large flat portobello mushrooms (allow 1 per person)
18 scallops, roe removed (allow 3 scallops per person)
cracked black pepper
finely diced tomato flesh, optional

Mix butter and chopped herbs then paint the mushrooms liberally in this herb butter and roast in a hot oven (175°C for 12 minutes) until cooked. Keep warm.

Pat scallops dry then dip the top and bottom of each in a little of the herb butter and season with cracked black pepper.

Heat a black searing pan until very hot and smoking. Place the scallops in the pan and sear quickly, 20-30 seconds per side, then place 3 scallops onto each warm mushroom. Dot the Beurre Blanc (recipe follows) around the plate. If desired, garnish with finely diced tomato flesh to add a little crunch to the dish.

Place a container of Double Mushroom Custard (see below) on each plate and serve immediately, while still warm.

Perfect with a Tasmanian Pinot Noir.

DOUBLE MUSHROOM CUSTARD
120g dried ceps
70g dried mixed 'forest' mushrooms
2 litres water
600ml cream
400ml whole milk
1 onion, finely diced
5 egg yolks

Simmer mushrooms and water for 15 minutes, stand for an extra 15 minutes off the heat. Strain liquid (reserving mushrooms) and reduce over medium heat by half (to approximately 1 litre). Add cream and milk to mushroom stock. Sweat the strained mushrooms and onion in a pan, cooking well over moderate heat but do not brown. Add to cream and stock mixture.

To make custard, take one cup of creamy stock and, in a heated double boiler, whisk in the egg yolks. Continue stirring over moderate heat until custard thickens and coats the back of a spoon. Pour into six small containers and keep warm until serving.

BEURRE BLANC
300g sliced shallots
2 tablespoons light olive oil
2 tablespoons Dijon mustard
200ml dry white wine
1 litre (4 cups) pouring cream
1 tablespoon dry white wine, extra
200g unsalted butter, cut into small cubes
salt to season

Sweat shallots in olive oil. Add mustard and wine then slowly whisk in the cream. Cook over low heat to reduce by 25 per cent. Strain, cool and refrigerate. Take 2 tablespoons of the reduction and heat over a double boiler, add extra white wine and a few knobs of the butter at a time, whisking all the time until desired consistency is attained. Season to taste with salt and add more mustard if necessary.

Don Cameron, Stillwater River Cafe, Launceston

Salads

This highly adaptable, tasty recipe includes the health benefits of hazelnuts and dark leafy raw vegetables. Vegetarians may wish to leave out the bacon, and add garlic, onion or capsicum. Vanessa Cox prepares this often, varying the ingredients according to who's going to be eating it.

WARM HAZELNUT SALAD   Serves 4

Approx 4 cups seasonal greens, such as spinach, swiss chard, beetroot leaves, warrigal greens (native spinach), stalks removed, washed and drained

3 lean bacon rashers, chopped to 2-3cm pieces

4-6 mushrooms, skinned and roughly chopped

1 dessertspoon olive oil (optional)

100g dry-roasted hazelnuts

Roughly chop or tear greens into pieces and place in serving bowl. Grill or fry bacon until crisp. Remove from pan and set aside in a warm oven. Retain bacon fat in the pan, or if you prefer discard and use olive oil.

Add the roughly chopped mushrooms to the fat or oil and fry until just tender. Shortly before serving, add the roast hazelnuts to the pan and heat with the mushrooms to bring out the full flavour. Drain off oil or fat, add the hot bacon pieces, and while still hot pour over the raw leaves, toss and serve immediately.

NOTE: For a sustaining main meal serve this salad on a bed of hot pasta, rice or couscous.

TIPS FOR SUCCESS

- Ensure the fresh, washed, drained, green leaves are stem free and dry before adding the hot ingredients. Serve within 2-5 minutes for maximum fresh flavours without leaf 'melt-down'.
- Olive oil is not essential. If the bacon renders enough fat (and there are no health issues) retain some or all bacon fat to maximise flavour in the warm ingredients.

Vanessa Cox, Mudgee Gourmet Hazelnuts, Mudgee

We reduce a 750ml bottle of red wine down to about 250ml and add 100g sugar,' says Pettavel Winery chef Richard Hooper. 'We then add more depending on how it's tasting and the viscosity. The sugar gives it a lovely sheen and it is not dribbling everywhere over the plate.'

MEREDITH EWE'S MILK FETA, WALNUT & APPLE SALAD with RED WINE DRESSING

Serves 6

2 Granny Smith apples, peeled, cored and cut into 5mm dice
1 cup shelled fresh walnuts, chopped very finely
1 small red onion, diced very finely
50ml red wine dressing
salt and pepper to taste
120g Meredith ewe's milk feta
2 cups small green salad leaves, frissee or watercress, washed and dried
30ml red wine reduction
(Heat red wine in a saucepan until it has reduced by two-thirds. Bottle and use as desired).

Mix the apple, walnut and red onion in a large bowl with half of the red wine dressing and sprinkle with a little salt and pepper. Mix until the dressing has coated all of the ingredients. Crumble the feta over, then mix well, tasting and adding more salt and pepper if desired. In a separate bowl, use the remaining red wine dressing to dress the salad leaves.

To serve the salad, place half of the leaves on to the plate, add a scoop of the feta mixture and top off the salad with the remaining leaves. To finish, drizzle red wine reduction lightly and evenly over the entire salad.

Richard Hooper, Pettavel Winery and Restaurant, Waurn Ponds

'This dish was put together using the five-point philosophy of my restaurant, that is: fresh, local, seasonal, simple, and stylish,' says Aaron Turner. 'The figs and capsicum are from a local market gardener, Sam Radone. The olive oil for the dill-infused oil is from Manzanillo Olive Grove in Drysdale, 4 kilometres away.'

FIG & PROSCIUTTO SALAD   Serves 4

1 red capsicum
½ bunch dill
100ml extra virgin olive oil
6 large fresh figs
8 slices prosciutto
200g rocket

Roast red capsicum in a hot oven, 200°C, until the skin has browned and starts to bubble. Remove from the oven and cover with foil, then allow to cool. This helps with the peeling of the capsicum. Reserve 4 sprigs of dill for garnish, place the remaining dill in a pan and cover with the oil.

Place the pan on the lowest heat available, and slowly heat the oil for 15 minutes. Remove and allow to cool. Stand 4 figs upright and make 2 diagonal cuts into the top of each fig to about a third of the way down each fig. Place your thumb and forefingers at the bottom of the fig and gently squeeze so that the incisions open up to reveal the flesh.

Cut the last 2 figs in half. Place a half fig as the base and the full fig on top. Lay out a slice of prosciutto and place a fig stack at one end on its side and wrap the prosciutto around it. Repeat with remaining fig stacks.

Peel the skin from the cooked capsicum, make an incision from top to bottom and open out flat. De-seed the capsicum, and cut into 4 large squares. Place a slice of capsicum on the plate, then some rocket leaves, then the prosciutto wrapped fig on top of the rocket. Drizzle some of the dill-infused oil around the dish and serve garnished with a sprig of dill.

Aaron Turner, Julian's Restaurant at Bellarine, Bellarine

Bellarine Estate Sauvignon Blanc 2004 is a perfect wine to enjoy with this dish.

This stunning, simple salad stunning uses local Yandoit walnuts, olive oil from the Orchard of St Francis and Lavandula figs. 'Cheese and salad are good to start a meal, to loosen the palate for what is to come,' says Jess Scarce. 'The ingredients are perfect late summer flavours, and complement each other.'

JESS'S FRESH FIG SALAD   Serves 4-6

3 cups rocket, stems removed
6 green figs, ideally fresh from the garden, sliced in rounds
½ cup marsala walnuts (see below)
shaved pecorino cheese
extra virgin olive oil
sea salt

Arrange the rocket and figs in two layers to give height. Top with walnuts and cheese. Drizzle over extra virgin olive oil, preferably from Rose Creek Estate, Colmo's Paddock or Orchard of St Francis, and season with a light sprinkle of sea salt.

MARSALA WALNUTS

100g butter
100g soft brown sugar
100ml marsala
2 cups walnut halves

Melt butter, add brown sugar and marsala and stir to combine. Add walnuts, tossing to coat well. Heat together over a low heat for 5 minutes. Cool.

Jess Scarce, La Trattoria, Lavandula, Shepherd's Flat

'Blackcurrants, in season late-December to mid-January, add a real zing to salads,' says Deborah Cantrill. 'They are my favourite but not many people seem to know what to do with them. They make a green salad special. Use raspberry or blackcurrant vinegar as a dressing.'

BLACKCURRANT GARDEN SALAD   Serves 4

2 cups lettuce and other salad greens
½ cup fresh green peas or beans
2 chopped spring onions
¼ cup fresh blackcurrants
1–2 tablespoons raspberry or black-currant vinegar, preferably Nirvana

Toss the first four ingredients together in a salad bowl and sprinkle with the raspberry or blackberry vinegar. Serve immediately.

Deborah Cantrill, Nirvana Organic Produce, Heathfield

'A simple salad. We often liked raw grated beetroot with salad dressing, but this is better,' says Deborah Cantrill. 'We make it when we have lots of beetroot fresh from the garden.'

RED ON RED SALAD   Serves 2

1 cup coarsely grated raw beetroot
1–2 tablespoons raspberry vinegar, preferably Nirvana

Place grated beetroot in salad bowl, toss in raspberry vinegar and serve.

Deborah Cantrill, Nirvana Organic Produce, Heathfield

'This recipe was an adaptation of a mixture used to make Vietnamese spring rolls. We have found it to be one of the most popular salads that we serve, and although not quite as crunchy the next day, it is still equally delicious.'

ASIAN RED CABBAGE SALAD   Serves 18

1 red cabbage, quartered, central
stem removed
1 cup fresh parsley
1 cup fresh coriander
½ cup fresh mint
½ cup Vietnamese mint or basil
1 cup slivered almonds, toasted

DRESSING
2½ tablespoons sesame oil
100ml lemon juice
2 tablespoon brown sugar
2½ tablespoons fish sauce
2½ tablespoons sweet chilli sauce
1 tablespoon minced ginger

Finely slice cabbage. Wash and roughly chop fresh herbs. Place cabbage in a large mixing bowl and combine with chopped herbs. Combine two thirds of the almonds with the cabbage mixture. Combine dressing ingredients and mix well through the salad. Sprinkle the remaining almonds over the salad and serve.

Annabelle Abbotts, Mt Hart Wilderness Lodge, Kimberley

Soups

Farmhouse in the mist, Yackandandah, Victoria.

The flavour of this traditional dish comes from the prawn shells and the tomalley in the heads. This version was developed for the Bisque and Chowder class at the Sydney Seafood School and is so popular that it appears on every program. Roberta Muir advises using green (raw, uncooked) shells and heads and mashing them well while cooking to extract as much flavour as possible.

PRAWN BISQUE   Serves 6

100g butter
1 onion, chopped
750g green prawn shells and heads
(from about 24 large prawns)
½ cup plain flour
1 cup white wine
1 litre (4 cups) water
½ cup cream
salt and freshly ground white pepper,
to taste
1 tablespoon brandy
a little extra cream
1 bunch chervil or chives,
finely chopped

Melt butter in a large saucepan and saute onion until soft. Add prawn heads and fry until they turn red. Crush prawn heads with a meat mallet or wooden spoon as they are frying—it is important that heads are crushed as much as possible.

Add flour and stir over medium heat for 3-5 minutes until flour is cooked out. Add wine and stir for a minute, then add water and bring to the boil. Reduce heat and simmer gently for 20-30 minutes.

Strain, pushing through a fine sieve to extract as much liquid as possible from the shells. Discard solids, and pass soup through a muslin cloth to remove any remaining solids. Return soup to a clean pan, add cream and simmer to heat through. Taste and season if necessary. Add brandy just before serving and stir through.

Serve with a swirl of fresh cream and garnish with some chopped chervil or chives.

Roberta Muir, Sydney Seafood School, Pyrmont

SEE PICTURE on page 60

This soup, like all of the recipes Paul Benhaim creates, is based on natural living foods. Paul (below) buys direct from local organic farmers and farming co-operatives to ensure the food is in its most natural state. 'These foods continue to astonish people as to how tasty simple, natural foods can be,' he says.

SOUPER BEET SOUP   Serves 2

1 fresh beetroot, cut into chunks
1 carrot, cut into chunks
1 tomato, roughly chopped
2 cups water
3 strawberries (optional)
1 small spring onion (optional)

Blend all ingredients in a mixer. If required, add water to desired consistency. Swirl in a generous helping of Macadamia Creme (see below).

MACADAMIA CREME
15 raw macadamia nuts
1 teaspoon hemp oil (contact Alive Foods for stockists, see page 166) or other organic oil
juice of 1 orange
3 fresh dates, pitted

Blend all ingredients in a food processor. Great as is, in a smoothie or dolloped into Souper Beet Soup.

Paul Benhaim, Alive Foods, Montville

This recipe was developed for The Herb Barn by celebrity chef Bart Beek of Essence Food Studio. The '30 seconds' poached salmon is served in a Japanese style broth and seasoned with sansho pepper and herb tea.

POACHED SALMON in CITRUS TWIST BROTH with SANSHO PEPPER

Serves 12

2 tablespoons The Herb Barn Citrus Twist Tea or other citrus tea
1 litre (4 cups) boiling water
1 teaspoon instant dashi (Japanese stock, available from supermarkets and Asian groceries)
2 tablespoons light soy sauce
1 tablespoon dark soy sauce
1 tablespoon mirin
1 tablespoon sugar
1 teaspoon salt flakes
1 small birds-eye chilli, seeds removed and finely sliced
1 thumb size piece fresh ginger, peeled and grated
12 pieces Atlantic salmon approx 125g each
½ cup roughly chopped coriander leaves
sansho** pepper to taste (available from Asian groceries)

Place Herb Barn Citrus Twist tea into a plunger and cover with boiling water. Let infuse for several minutes then pour the strained tea into a saucepan. Add all the remaining ingredients except salmon, coriander and sansho pepper. Bring to a boil then turn down to a gentle simmer. Keep warm until required. Steam salmon in a steamer for 30 seconds and transfer to small individual tasting bowls. Ladle over some of the hot strained broth, garnish with coriander, season with the sansho pepper, and serve immediately.

Suzy Martin, The Herb Barn Pty Ltd, Tatong

CURRIED ZUCCHINI & SWEET POTATO SOUP
with COCONUT MILK   Serves 6

2 large onions, chopped
1 tablespoon olive oil
500g zucchini, roughly chopped
500g sweet potato, peeled and
roughly chopped
1 tablespoon good curry powder
1 tablespoon
vegetable stock powder
water
400g can coconut milk

Fry onions in olive oil until golden, add other vegetables and sweat gently over a low heat for five minutes. Add curry and stock powder with enough water to cover. Bring to the boil, then simmer until very soft (approximately 45 minutes). Blend with a stick blender (or use a food processor), then return to the pan. Add the coconut milk, and gently reheat.

Lynette Klavins, Penna Lane Wines, Clare

Enjoy with Penna Lane Wines 2005 Rambling Rosé.

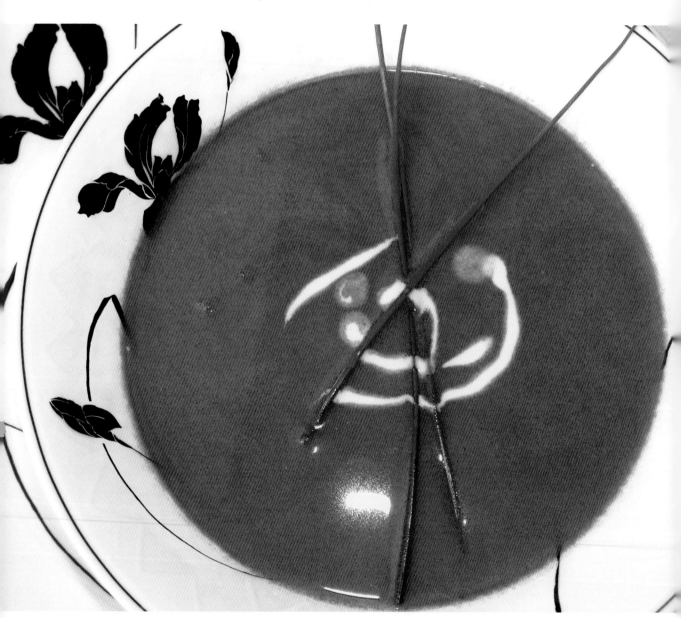

Prawn Bisque (see page 56 for recipe)

'At Penna Lane Wines we do many varieties of interesting condiments and simple lunches,' says Lynette Klavins. 'In winter, hearty soup is our speciality. These soups are rich and very thick—and each is a meal on its own. I serve them with home-baked bread.'

MOROCCAN SPICED CHICKPEA & ROASTED PUMPKIN SOUP

Serves 6–8

400g dried chickpeas, soaked overnight
1 small whole round pumpkin, such as Australian Butter or Queensland Blue
3 large onions, chopped
1 tablespoon ground cumin
1 tablespoon ground coriander
1 tablespoon ground turmeric
2 tablespoons vegetable stock powder
Greek yoghurt
cracked pepper to serve

Discard the soaking water from the chickpeas, place them in a saucepan and cover with fresh water. Bring to the boil, then reduce heat and cook gently until very tender (at least an hour). Place the pumpkin whole on an oven tray and roast in a moderate oven until quite soft (about an hour). Leave until cool enough to handle.

Cut the pumpkin open and, with a spoon, remove the seeds and discard, then scrape out the flesh into a large saucepan. Add the chickpeas and their cooking water, the onions, spices, stock powder and enough extra water to cover. Bring to the boil, then simmer for an hour. Blend with a stick blender (or place in a food processor) then reheat. Serve with a grinding of black pepper and a dollop of thick Greek yoghurt.

Lynette Klavins , Penna Lane Wines, Clare

Enjoy with Penna Lane Wines 2004 Semillion.

Mains

This dish is typical of the many new delicacies Stephen Neale comes up with and shows his preference for fresh, in-season foods.

CRISPY SKIN NATIVE SILVER PERCH   Serves 4

115g green beans
115g baby asparagus
450g kipfler potatoes, washed not peeled
4 x 115g native silver perch fillets
salt and ground black pepper
HOW MUCH ??? salad leaves
1 red onion, sliced
115g cherry tomatoes, halved
4 tablespoons black olives
2 pickled quail's eggs, drained and halved (Dawn's recommended)
lime salad dressing
(Available from selected delicatessens.)
saffron mayonnaise

Blanch beans and asparagus in boiling water, then refresh in cold water. Cook potatoes in boiling salted water for approximately 15 minutes. Drain and set aside. Season perch fillets with salt and ground black pepper then cook skin side down on a very hot griddle pan brushed with a little olive oil. Turn over after three minutes or when the skin is golden in colour. Continue to cook for a further three minutes on second side.

Toss the salad leaves, beans, asparagus, onion, tomato, potatoes and olives in lime dressing and arrange on the plates. Place four quail egg halves around the salad, then top with perch fillets. Drizzle some saffron mayonnaise (made by mixing saffron and pureed garlic with a whole egg mayonnaise) around the plate.

Stephen Neale, Three Snails Restaurant, Dubbo

'This recipe is what Cowra has been known for—great lamb-producing country,' say Anna Wong and Jerry Mouzakis.

COWRA LAMB RUMP
WITH SPICY DU PUY LENTILS & ROAST PUMPKIN   Serves 4

180g du puy lentils
1 tablespoon olive oil
Maldon sea salt
1 medium brown onion, finely chopped
1 small chilli, deseeded and finely chopped
2 garlic cloves, peeled and finely chopped
4 large sprigs thyme
1 teaspoon smoked Spanish paprika
80ml (4 tablespoons) chardonnay
800g can peeled Roma tomatoes (or fresh blanched and peeled tomatoes, if in season)
salt and pepper to taste
100g sheep's milk or natural yoghurt
extra tablespoon olive oil
1 butternut pumpkin, peeled and cut into 3cm slices
4 lamb rumps (250g each, trimmed— Mulligan Cowra recommended)
120ml (½ cup) veal jus
black pepper
fresh watercress

Place the lentils in a small saucepan and cover with cold water. Bring to the boil and strain. Repeat this process three times until the water is relatively clear.

Heat a large saucepan on a low flame, add some olive oil and a pinch of sea salt. When the oil is lightly smoking add the onion, chilli, garlic, thyme and paprika, stirring continuously until the mixture caramelises and begins to stick to the bottom of the pot. Deglaze the pot with the chardonnay and remove the thyme. Add the tomatoes and reduce this mixture by half, then add the lentils. Season to taste with salt and pepper.

Place yoghurt in a bowl and season with salt, pepper and olive oil, whisking with each addition. Roast pumpkin in a preheated 230°C oven with extra olive oil until cooked. Season lamb rumps and sear in a pan on a high heat with some olive oil until golden brown. Transfer to a hot oven for 8 minutes, then allow to rest in a warm place for five minutes.

Slice and serve with roasted pumpkin, lentils, watercress, yoghurt and veal jus. Season to taste with sea salt and black pepper.

Anna Wong and Jerry Mouzakis, Neila Restaurant, Cowra

'Our recipes aim to achieve an equilibrium of flavours and textures,' say Anna Wong and Jerry Mouzakis. 'The red dates are crunchy and sweet while the venison itself is salty and soft, balancing the mix.'

SICHUAN PEPPER & SOY CURED VENISON & CHINESE RED DATE SALAD
Serves 4–6

500g venison fillet
(can also use Wagyu beef)

CURING MIX
1 part each:
rock sugar
salt
Sichuan peppercorns
coriander roots
light soy sauce

SALAD DRESSING
1 chilli, deseeded
2 garlic cloves
2cm piece ginger, peeled
1 tablespoon sesame seeds
100ml (5 tablespoons) olive oil
1 ½ tablespoons sesame oil
2 ½ tablespoons light soy sauce
lemon juice to taste

CHINESE RED DATE SALAD
8–12 fresh Chinese red dates
4 cups red shisso leaves
small bunch chives
handful Thai basil
handful mint leaves
1 cup julienned carrot
pickled daikon to taste

Clean and cut venison into long thin pieces. Combine all of the dry Curing Mix ingredients and grind together in a mortar and pestle. Sprinkle venison liberally with the curing mix and leave 24 hours in the refrigerator to cure.

Wipe excess curing mix from venison and sear quickly in a very hot pan on all sides then place in refrigerator until needed.

For dressing, blend chilli, garlic and ginger in a blender. Fry this mix and the sesame seeds in olive oil until the mixture is fragrant, then allow to cool. Whisk in the sesame oil and light soy and season with lemon juice. Slice venison finely.

Slice or shred all salad ingredients and mix together. Toss venison, salad mix and dressing together and serve immediately.

Anna Wong and Jerry Mouzakis, Neila Restaurant, Cowra

Fromagebelle is a fresh curd cheese that can be used in any recipe that requires ricotta, sour cream or cream cheese. 'When I get frazzled and run off my feet going to farmers' markets, Mum makes me this dish and brings it to the markets so I don't have to cook on the weekends,' says Kate Woodward

FROMAGEBELLE & SPINACH CANNELLONI   Serves 4–6

250g spinach, raw, finely shredded
225g Fromagebelle
2 egg yolks
1 garlic clove, crushed
¾ cup grated cheese
nutmeg
salt
pepper
125g instant cannelloni tubes
2 tablespoons oil
425g canned tomatoes, pureed
1 teaspoon dried basil

Combine spinach, Fromagebelle, egg yolks, garlic, ¼ cup of grated cheese, some nutmeg and salt in a bowl. Fill dry cannelloni tubes with this mixture. In a pan, cook oil, canned tomatoes, basil and salt and pepper to taste until boiling. Remove from heat. Pour half the tomato sauce in a dish then place a layer of the filled cannelloni tubes. Pour over the remaining sauce and sprinkle with ½ cup of grated cheese. Bake in a preheated 200°C oven for 30–35 min. Test with a skewer to check if cooked.

Kate Woodward, Hunter Belle Cheese, Muswellbrook

Bradley Teale sources his duck from local suppliers, Redgate Farm, at nearby Woodville.

ROASTED SOY DUCK with
STEAMED SPICED EGGPLANT & TATSOI SALAD   Serves 4

100ml kecap manis
(sweet soy sauce,
available from Asian grocers)
1 teaspoon sesame oil
2 tablespoons boiling water
1 No 18 duck
knob garlic, roughly cut
knob ginger, roughly cut
1 star anise
sea salt and freshly ground black
pepper
200g water chestnuts, roughly sliced
¼ bunch spring onions, sliced finely
diagonally
tatsoi salad leaves

Mix kecap manis, sesame oil and water together. Remove the neck of the duck, wings to the knuckle closest to the bird, knuckle from the leg, and fat from within the cavity, reserving for another use, if desired. Place the garlic and ginger in the duck's cavity with the star anise and some salt and pepper. Quarter-fill a roasting pan with water and place a rectangular cake rack over it. Place the duck onto it and brush with half the kecap manis mixture.

Season and roast in a preheated 220°C oven for 20 minutes. Reduce oven heat to 200°C and roast for around 50 minutes or until completely cooked, while basting regularly with the remaining kecap manis mixture and liquid in the tray. Allow to cool, then cut or break the duck into breast and Maryland pieces, removing the thigh bone and any extra fat.

To serve, place the four duck pieces in a preheated 200°C oven for 10 minutes or until hot. Warm steamed spiced eggplant (recipe follows) in a saucepan, remove from stove and fold in water chestnuts, spring onions and half the black vinegar dressing (recipe follows). Place steamed spiced eggplant in the centre of each of four plates, scatter with tatsoi, then top with a heated duck portion and drizzle with more dressing.

STEAMED SPICED EGGPLANT

½ teaspoon fennel seeds
½ teaspoon Sichuan peppercorns
2 large eggplants,
cut in large (2cm) dice
salt
1 teaspoon finely chopped garlic
1 tablespoon finely chopped ginger
canola oil for sauteing
1 tablespoon
Chinese Shaoxing rice wine
1 tablespoon rice vinegar
1 ½ tablespoons light soy sauce
1 tablespoon chicken stock
1 tablespoon castor sugar
2 teaspoons sesame oil
2 teaspoons fish sauce

Dry fry fennel seeds and peppercorns until fragrant. Cool and grind to a powder. Sprinkle eggplant cubes with salt and allow to drain for 30 minutes. Pat dry and steam for 30 minutes or until cooked. Briefly saute garlic and ginger in canola oil, add the ground spices and saute briefly. Add all remaining ingredients (except eggplant), bring to the boil, simmer for 3 minutes, then add the eggplant and fold into sauce. Put aside until serving time.

BLACK VINEGAR DRESSING

1 tablespoon finely chopped ginger
2 tablespoons chopped coriander
stems
2 tablespoons kecap manis
2 tablespoons black vinegar
(available from Asian grocers)
1 tablespoon sesame oil
1 ½ tablespoons light soy sauce
¼ teaspoon chilli oil

Mix all ingredients together well.

Bradley Teale, Esca Bimbadgen, Pokolbin

This is one of Warren Thompson's signature dishes.

TEMPURA NORI ROLLED ATLANTIC SALMON
with BLUE SWIMMER CRAB & GINGER MOUSSE   Serves 6

180g Enoki & Crab Mousse
(recipe below)
12 x 90g Atlantic salmon fillets
6 sheets nori paper
flour
1 packet tempura batter
(available from Asian grocers)
900ml kombu broth
1 bunch shallots, ⅔ cut as batons
and blanched, ⅓ julienned
300g enoki mushrooms

Prepare Crab Mousse and Kombu Broth first.

Divide Blue Swimmer Crab and Ginger Mousse (see below) between half the salmon fillets, spreading on smoothly. Place remaining fillets on top to make a 'sandwich'. Place nori sheets on a table flaky side up, brush with water, place a salmon stack on each and roll up. Dredge with flour and dip in batter, then fry in a deep fryer for 3–4 minutes or until golden. Rest, cut into three. Place three rounds in a wide bowl with hot kombu broth and blanched shallots, and enoki mushrooms and shallot julienne for garnish.

BLUE SWIMMER CRAB
& GINGER MOUSSE

200g picked blue swimmer
crab meat
2 egg whites
300ml cream
1 teaspoon sea salt
fresh ginger, peeled and finely diced
200g enoki mushrooms, blanched
and chopped

In a chilled food processor bowl, pulse the crab meat, then add egg whites. Pour on approximately 200ml cream, beat until soft peaks. Pass through a fine sieve into a bowl resting on ice. Mix in 100 ml cream. Season with salt (this helps tighten the mousse) and finish with ginger and enoki mushrooms. Chill until needed

KOMBU BROTH

Dashi (see below)
200 ml Japanese soy
250 ml mirin
50ml tamari
100g bonito flakes

Prepare Dashi first. In each recipe bring all ingredients except bonito nearly to the boil, but do not allow to boil. Remove immediately from the heat, add bonito and allow to infuse before straining.

DASHI

3.6 litres water
50g kombu
80g bonito flakes
(All available from Asian grocers)

Warren Thompson, Big Fish, Shoal Bay Resort & Spa, Shoal Bay

This property specialises in small batch specialty cheeses, so naturally this recipe features cheese!

THREE CHEESE TORTA with CARAMELISED ONION & ROASTED PUMPKIN

Serves 4

500g ricotta
⅓ cup almond meal
½ cup grated parmesan
1 garlic clove, crushed
salt and pepper
500g butternut pumpkin, halved lengthways, peeled, de-seeded and cut into 1cm slices
1 red onion, cut into thin wedges leaving base intact
brown sugar
2 tablespoons extra virgin olive oil
salt and freshly ground pepper
150g drained feta, crumbled
2 tablespoons shredded fresh basil

Preheat oven to 180°C. Lightly grease four 10cm loose-bottomed, non-stick tart pans. Place the ricotta in a bowl with almond meal, parmesan and garlic and season with salt and pepper. Mix together well, then press the mixture into the tart pans, place on a baking tray and bake for 20 minutes or until puffed and golden.

Meanwhile, place pumpkin, onion, a little brown sugar and oil in an oven bag separately. Toss to combine and season with salt and pepper. Place on racks in oven until pumpkin is tender and browned .

To serve, pile onion and pumpkin on top of cooked tortas. A high presentation looks best, but don't overload. Scatter with feta and basil.

Grosvenor and Ro Francis, John Grant,
High Valley Wine & Cheese, Mudgee

DAVIDSON PLUM LAMB with BUSH SPICES   Serves 4

500–800g rolled lamb loin (or use lamb chops)
½ teaspoon ground lemon myrtle
½ teaspoon dry mustard
½ teaspoon ground ginger
¼ teaspoon tabasco sauce
1 tablespoon soy sauce
1 cup Davidson Plum Jam or Davidson Plum Chilli Sauce
½ teaspoon ground Dorrigo pepper
¼ cup onion, diced finely
½ teaspoon ground aniseed myrtle

Place lamb in a baking dish. In a small bowl, mix together all of the other ingredients. Pour over lamb. Bake lamb, uncovered, in a 200°C oven until meat is cooked, about 30–40 minutes (20–25 min for lamb chops).

Serve lamb with plum jam or plum chilli sauce on top.

Barbara Barlin, Barbushco Pty Ltd, Lorne

LEMON MYRTLE & MACADAMIA GREEN SEAFOOD CURRY   Serves 2

1 tablespoon canola oil
1 tablespoon green curry paste
1 tablespoon macadamia nut paste
2 teaspoons Dorrigo pepper
1 teaspoon rainforest blend spice
1 small tin coconut cream
½ head broccoli, cut in florets
1 teaspoon ground lemon myrtle
400g white fish
1 bunch bok choy, quartered
4 large green prawns, shelled and deveined
1 squid tube, sliced in rings
cooked jasmine rice
2 sprigs coriander

Heat oil in pan, add curry paste and macadamia paste in oil and stir until aromatic. Add Dorrigo pepper and rainforest blend spice and stir. Add coconut cream and bring to the boil and stir, then broccoli, lemon myrtle and fish. Simmer for 5 minutes. Add bok choy, prawns and squid and simmer for 1 more minute.

Serve with steamed jasmine rice or rice steamed with a couple of dried whole lemon myrtle leaves. Top with coriander sprigs.

Barbara Barlin, Barbushco Pty Ltd, Lorne

'Manning Valley beef is produced under strict regulation and is 'natural'', says Wolfgang Zichy.

GRILLED MANNING VALLEY NATURAL BEEF FILLET topped with a THREE MUSTARD SAUCE, served with BABY BEETROOT, SNOW PEAS & GARLIC POTATO MASH

Serves 4

4 beef fillets (around 300g each), silver membrane and fat trimmed off

1½ tablespoons extra virgin olive oil

2 brown onions, finely chopped

3 garlic cloves, crushed

150ml fresh cream

1 tablespoon each wholegrain, hot English and Dijon mustard, or as preferred

4 baby beetroot

200ml orange juice

8 medium potatoes, peeled and cut into small pieces

5 garlic cloves, peeled

freshly ground salt and pepper

pinch of nutmeg

1 tablespoon butter

100ml hot full cream milk

24 snow peas, topped and tailed

On a very hot grill, seal the beef fillet for a minute on either side, set aside. Heat oil in large pan, add onions and garlic and saute, but do not allow to colour. Add cream and mustards, stir and let simmer for 20 minutes. Keep warm. Boil beetroot until just tender, refresh in cold water and peel when cool enough to handle, then cut in halves.

Bring orange juice to the boil, add beetroot and simmer until heated through. Boil potatoes with garlic, salt, pepper and nutmeg, and when soft, strain, add butter and milk and mash into a soft puree. Season with salt, pepper and nutmeg.

Blanch the snow peas for two minutes in a pot of boiling water. Drain, brush with a little olive oil, and keep warm. To finish off the beef, put fillets on a tray in a preheated 220°C oven, and bake to your liking (well done 20 minutes, medium 15 minutes, rare 8–12 minutes, blue around 5 minutes from room temperature).

To serve, place a good tablespoon of mashed potato on each warmed plate, place beef fillet on top, arrange beetroot and snow peas around the plate, ladle mustard sauce over the fillet. Serve immediately.

Wolfgang Zichy, The Moorings Restaurant and Cafe, Harrington

Moorings recommends Tempus Two 2003 Cannonball Cabernet Merlot.

Matthew Wild says this dish showcases fresh, local Yamba prawns. 'The textures of the three food combinations—the prawns, the peasant-style braise and the tang of the saffron mayonnaise—make this a well-executed dish which explodes in an array of flavours in the mouth.'

CHAR-GRILLED YAMBA PRAWNS, TOMATO, FENNEL & OLIVE BRAISE with SAFFRON MAYONNAISE

Serves 6

4 fennel bulbs, sliced
2 brown onions, sliced
6 garlic cloves, finely chopped
125ml good quality olive oil
500g whole peeled tomatoes, crushed
½ cup pitted black olives, sliced
pinch Maldon sea salt
pinch ground black pepper
18 Yamba prawns, cleaned
2½ tablespoons melted butter for basting
½ bunch flat leaf parsley, finely chopped
good quality olive oil, extra

Put fennel, onion and garlic in olive oil in a heavy baking dish. Add crushed tomatoes and black olives. Braise for 2 hours on low heat. Sprinkle with Maldon sea salt and pepper. Cover and store until required.

Baste Yamba prawns with butter on a hot char-grill until cooked. Place prawns on braise; dress with saffron mayonnaise (recipe follows), parsley and a splash of a good quality olive oil.

SAFFRON MAYONNAISE

1 egg
1 cup salad oil
1 teaspoon Dijon mustard
Maldon sea salt, to taste
2 teaspoons lemon juice
5 saffron strands, pounded and soaked

Place all ingredients in a jug and blend with a hand blender until mayonnaise thickens.

Matthew Wild, Wild at Byron, The Byron at Byron, Byron Bay

Left: Near Bellingen, New South Wales.

'My wife, who has always played a huge part in writing my menus, loves risotto and I love barbecue duck,' admits chef Robert Salmon. 'This keeps us both happy. I often run this dish as a special in my restaurant.'

CHINESE BARBECUED DUCK RISOTTO   Serves 6

1 Chinese barbecued duck (available from Asian butchers)
1½ litres chicken or duck stock
3 tablespoons vegetable oil
3 garlic cloves, finely chopped
3 sticks lemongrass, finely chopped
1 large onion, diced
2 tablespoons finely chopped ginger
1 tablespoon five spice
2 cups arborio rice
2 tablespoons sherry
2 tablespoons sweet soy
2 tablespoons hoisin sauce
2 tablespoons oyster sauce
½ cup coriander, chopped
8 shallots, sliced diagonally
6 dried Chinese mushrooms (soaked in hot water until soft. Drain and cut off stems and slice.)
fish sauce, to taste

De-bone the duck, keeping meat separate from the skin and all the bones. Cut the meat up into medium size pieces.

If you don't want to use chicken stock, you can make a duck stock with the skin and bones. Make this a day ahead as you'll want it to completely cool so you can skim off all the fat before use.

Heat the stock in a separate pot and turn off when boiling. Heat the oil and saute the garlic, lemongrass, onion and ginger slowly without colouring, until soft. Add five spice and rice. The rice will begin to lightly fry so keep stirring. Once the rice looks slightly translucent add the hot stock, one ladle at a time. Turn the heat down to a gentle simmer.

Keep stirring the rice, and when the stock has been completely absorbed each time, add the next ladle of stock. This should take about 15 minutes until all the stock is used or the right smooth and creamy consistency has been achieved.

Keep checking the rice to see if it is cooked. Once done, add the sherry, soy, hoisin and oyster sauces. Stir in well, then add all of the other ingredients except the fish sauce. Finally add the fish sauce to taste.

Robert Salmon, The Silos Restaurant, Jaspers Brush

Sheldon Wearne cooks this dish 5–10 times a night, it's so popular. It was created 'by making a mistake and adding to it,' he admits.

LIGHT CURRY-SPICED CORAL TROUT with WATERMELON SALSA & CRISPY SEAWEED

Serves 4

4 x 200g fresh coral trout fillets

Place fish fillets into a hot lightly oiled pan and cook to golden brown turning only once. Smear Curry Paste (recipe below) on top of each fish portion and place in hot oven for 3 minutes. To serve, place generous portion of Watermelon Salsa (recipe below) in the centre of each serving plate. Place fish fillet on top, curry side up, and garnish with Crispy Seaweed (recipe below).

CURRY PASTE

1 teaspoon cumin seeds, fennel seeds coriander seeds and sweet paprika
2 cardamom pods
2 cloves
100g tom yum paste
100ml vegetable oil
2 teaspoons sugar

Grind all spice ingredients to a powder in a spice mill and add to tom yum paste. Add oil slowly while mixing with spoon until the mixture becomes a smooth paste.

WATERMELON SALSA

1 onion, sliced
2 fresh chillies, chopped
½ cup snowpeas
2 tablespoons chopped coriander
1 tablespoon marinated hijiki seaweed (optional)
200g diced watermelon pieces, no seeds
juice of 2 limes

Add onion and chilli to a hot frying pan and cook until lightly browned. Add snowpeas, coriander, hijiki and diced watermelon and toss to heat. Add lime juice and fish sauce and simmer for 30 seconds.

CRISPY SEAWEED

100gm nori seaweed sheets
(all ingredients available from Asian grocers)

Use kitchen scissors to cut seaweed into thin strips. Deep fry strips for 30 seconds or until crispy.

Sheldon Wearne, 2 Fish Restaurant, Cairns and Port Douglas

TEMPURA GULF BUGS ON LEMONGRASS SKEWERS with GREEN PAPAYA SALAD, SWEET LEMON MYRTLE DIPPING SAUCE & TARO CHIPS

Serves 4

8 fresh lemongrass skewers
20 pieces of Gulf bug meat
1 packet tempura batter
(Available from Asian grocers)
1 litre vegetable oil for deep frying
1 taro, peeled and cut in 2mm slices
bottled sweet chilli lemon myrtle
dipping sauce, or similar

Cut lemongrass sticks on an angle at the point where stem starts to branch. Skewer two to three pieces of bug meat onto each stick of lemongrass. Prepare batter according to instructions. Heat oil to 180°C. Fry taro slices until crisp, then drain on paper towels. Dip bug skewers into prepared batter and fry until golden and cooked through.

Assemble Papaya Salad on plate, place skewers across, garnish with taro chips and serve with green papaya salad (recipe follows) and dipping sauce.

GREEN PAPAYA SALAD

1 green papaya, peeled, cut into long matchsticks
3 fresh small whole green chillies, finely sliced
3 cloves garlic, chopped roughly
6 long green beans, cut into 2.5 cm pieces
½ cup unsalted roasted peanuts
1 red onion, sliced
1 red capsicum, sliced
½ bunch mint, chopped
½ bunch coriander, chopped
3 tablespoons lime or lemon juice
1 tablespoon palm sugar
100ml fish sauce
1 teaspoon salt

Prepare papaya salad the day before. Mix all ingredients together and refrigerate until needed.

Craig Squire, Red Ochre Grill, Cairns

Tie the pork with twine to hold its shape or ask your butcher to put it in tight netting, suggests Craig Squire.

TWICE COOKED MAREEBA PORK SHOULDER with SPRING ONION RICE CAKE & TROPIC SPIRIT PINEAPPLE CHILLI JAM
Serves 4

4 x 300g pieces pork shoulder, skin off
600ml beef or veal stock
1 split chilli
15gm coriander stalk, bruised
2 star anise
⅓ cup castor sugar
150ml kecap manis
100ml rice vinegar
15g ginger, sliced
Tropic Spirit Pineapple Chilli Jam
(Available from Red Ochre Grill, Cairns.)

Place pork pieces in a roasting tray. Bring the remaining ingredients to a simmer in a saucepan and pour over pork when hot. Bake slowly in a preheated 130°C oven for about 90 minutes, turning often. Cool in liquid overnight. Remove from the set stock, and put aside. Reduce the stock, skimming off fat, until it reaches the desired flavour, then thicken slightly with cornflour and strain.

To serve, remove net or string from cooked pork pieces and warm up in a steamer for 15 minutes then place on a hot barbecue plate to brown lightly. Fry spring onion rice cakes (recipe below) in vegetable oil until golden. Serve sliced pork on rice cake, with Tropic Spirit Pineapple Chilli Jam and fresh coriander.

SPRING ONION RICE CAKE

200gm cooked rice short grain (a bit over-cooked is good)
1 shallot, sliced
1 egg white
2 cloves garlic
knob of ginger
¼ bunch coriander
1½ tablespoons sweet chilli sauce
salt and pepper to taste
cornflour to bind and coat

Mix all ingredients together well. With damp hands, form into patties, and coat well with cornflour before frying.

Craig Squire, Red Ochre Grill, Cairns

This recipe, based on the Batchjula people's way of cooking locally caught barramundi wrapped in paperbark sheets on open fire coals, was created at 'bush tukka' restaurant Seabelle. 'For success, fresh fish is a must. Tie the 'boat' ends tightly. This keeps in moisture and a delicate smoky flavour.'

BARRAMUNDI in PAPERBARK with FRAGRANT SALSA

Serves 4

For each main course serve:
200g skinless boneless barramundi fillet
25cm x 10cm piece of paperbark
20g whole macadamia nuts, lightly roasted until just coloured
butcher's twine
1 tablespoon melted butter
grilled lemon slice

Trim fish into a rectangle. Wet paperbark well then dab off excess moisture (this helps with rolling) and spread macadamia nuts on centre of paperbark. Place fish on nuts and roll long sides of paperbark in two or three small turns on each side. Gather in one end and tie with butcher's twine, then tie off the other end in the same manner. The end result should look like an old fashioned dhow boat. Drizzle with melted butter.

Place in a preheated 180°C for 15 minutes. At this time the fish should be soft to the touch, moist and just breaking apart if tested with a fork.

To serve, place fish 'boat' on a plate. Top with Fragrant Salsa and a hot grilled lemon slice. Accompany with your favourite crispy green salad and a glass of sauvignon blanc.

FRAGRANT SALSA

1 medium firm tomato, cut in small dice
½ medium Spanish onion, finely diced
1 tablespoon capers
4 lemon aspen, cut into quarters
2 tablespoons brown sugar
20ml balsamic vinegar
30ml olive oil, light
finely crushed sea salt
crushed black pepper (for a lovely difference, chopped green peppercorns can be substituted)
10g ground lemon myrtle
10g ground aniseed myrtle
(Both myrtles are carried at major supermarkets, growers' markets or can be found at www.cherikoff.net)

Mix all ingredients together well in a bowl. Add salt and pepper to taste. Chill before use.

Cort Assenheim, Seabelle Restaurant, Fraser Island

This is one of the recipes cooked during Annette Fear's stir fry classes and appears in Spirit House Thai Cooking. *The tartness of the pineapple blends well with the mild sweet flavour of the pork, creating a sweet and sour stir fry.*

STIR FRY OF PORK with PINEAPPLE, GINGER & YELLOW BEAN SAUCE
Serves 4

2 tablespoons vegetable oil

1 tablespoon chopped fresh garlic

500g pork fillet, chopped into small bite sized pieces

1 tablespoon finely shredded ginger

2 tablespoons yellow bean sauce

2 tablespoons oyster sauce

2 tablespoons palm sugar

1 red capsicum cut into thin strips

½ fresh pineapple, peeled, cored and cut into chunks

½ teaspoon freshly ground white peppercorns

½ bunch green onions, cut into long slices

Heat oil in wok until a moderate heat. Stir fry garlic briefly until golden. Turn heat to high. Add pork and ginger, and stir fry until pork starts to colour. Add yellow bean sauce, oyster sauce and palm sugar, stir frying until pork is cooked. Add capsicum and pineapple, stir fry for one minute. Add white pepper and green onions, toss briefly. Transfer to a serving platter, serve with steamed jasmine rice.

TIPS FOR SUCCESSFUL STIR FRYING

The secret to a successful stir fry is speed and heat. Never overcooked, the food should remain crunchy and full of flavour. Have all ingredients prepared and on hand next to the stove. Cooking time is minimal, once started, there is no time to suddenly remember you haven't chopped the garlic. Never cook more than 500 grams of meat at any one time. Have the wok very hot, otherwise the ingredients will start to 'stew'. Don't overcrowd the wok.

On a domestic wok burner, you can make a brilliant stir fry for 1–2 people, but the quality diminishes once you start to cook for more at any one time. So, if stir frying for large numbers, cook 2 serves first, put aside in a warm place, then quickly cook the next serve. When the food goes in to the wok, keep it moving. Remember, it is called a 'stir and fry', not a 'steam and stew'!

Use a good quality vegetable oil such as canola, peanut oil. Never use cold pressed oil, especially extra virgin olive oil because the fruitiness is incompatible with Asian flavours. Add a few drops of sesame oil to the finished dish for a delightfully nutty sesame flavour

Helen Brierty and Annette Fear, Spirit House Restaurant and Cooking School, Yandina

French-born chef Jerome Tremoulet (below) revels in the bounty of South Australian produce, seafood and meats, creating dishes to harmonise with Penfolds' prestigious wines. He suggests making the gratin and jus well ahead of baking the beef.

AGED BLACK ANGUS BEEF TENDERLOIN with BEEF CHEEK JUS, LEEK & POTATO GRATIN & GRAPE REDUCTION
Serves 4

4 x 120g pieces of aged Black Angus beef tenderloin

oil to sear

2 tablespoons fresh soy beans, or baby broad beans, blanched and skinned

4 baby leeks, blanched

4 cherry tomatoes

Sear the beef on both sides in oil in a very hot pan. Bake the beef in a preheated 200°C oven for 4 minutes.

To serve, place some Beef Cheek Jus (recipe follows) on each plate, top with rested tenderloin. Arrange a round of Leek and Potato Gratin (recipe follows) beside the meat and top with a cherry tomato and a baby leek. Scatter soya beans around the meat and the gratin.

BEEF CHEEK JUS

4 beef cheeks

vegetable oil

1 large carrot, chopped

1 large onion, chopped

1 piece celery, chopped

½ head garlic, peeled and chopped

1 leek, chopped

good sprig thyme

1 bay leaf

vegetable oil

200ml red wine

1.2 litres veal stock

500g red grapes

Sear the beef cheeks in a frying pan in vegetable oil until beginning to brown. Saute the chopped vegetables with the thyme and bay leaf in vegetable oil in a flameproof and ovenproof dish. Add the beef cheeks, then red wine and reduce by half. Add veal stock, bring to the boil, then cook in a preheated 200°C oven for 2½ hours. When the cheek is cooked add the grapes. Cook for about 1 hour on low heat, then pass the jus through a sieve. Keep warm or reheat at serving time.

LEEK AND POTATO GRATIN

4 large potatoes, peeled and thinly sliced
300ml cream
100ml milk
1 large white leek, chopped

Cook the potatoes in the cream and milk with the leek for 10 minutes over medium heat. Place the mix in a greased tray. Cook in a preheated 200°C oven for 45 minutes. Cool, then press down.

Jerome Tremoulet, Penfolds Magill Estate Restaurant, Magill

'We keep the Chilli Coriander Dressing on hand to use as a dipping sauce for sushi, cold rolls, fish—it's a really useful multi-purpose ingredient to have,' says chef Kas Martin.

SESAME CRUSTED CHICKEN with ASIAN SLAW & CHILLI CORIANDER DRESSING

Serves 6

6 small chicken breast fillets, trimmed and slightly flattened
1 egg, beaten with a splash of fish sauce
¼ cup plain flour
1 cup sesame seeds
salt and pepper
oil for frying
deep fried shallots
(available from Asian grocers)
fresh coriander

Dip flattened chicken into the egg and fish sauce mixture, draining off excess egg. Dip in flour, then sesame seeds, and season well. Refrigerate until required. When ready to cook, preheat oven to 180°C. Place coated chicken on a tray lined with silicone paper. Drizzle chicken with a little oil (canola is good). Bake for approximately 20 minutes or until cooked through. Leave to one side whilst preparing Asian Slaw (recipe follows).

To serve, place slaw on serving plates in equal amounts. Place chicken on top of slaw, leaving whole or cut in half, as you wish. Sprinkle over a little Chilli Coriander Dressing (recipe follows). Garnish with deep fried shallots and fresh coriander leaves.

ASIAN SLAW

½ small red cabbage, finely sliced
1 small red onion, finely sliced
10 snow peas, finely sliced
1 small carrot, julienned
100g bean sprouts finely shredded
mint leaves
chilli coriander dressing

Toss all slaw ingredients together well and mix through enough dressing to coat well.

CHILLI CORIANDER DRESSING

1 cup Yaldara verjus
½ cup white sugar
¾ cup white vinegar
¾ cup sweet chilli sauce
½ cup fish sauce
½ cup coriander, leaves and stems
2 cloves garlic
3 teaspoons sesame oil

Blend the dressing ingredients together. Taste and adjust if required. It should be a balance of flavours—neither too sweet nor too sharp. This amount of dressing will give enough for the salad and plenty left over to store in the fridge.

Kas Martin , Cafe Y, Yaldara Estates, Lyndoch

'This is our own recipe, created by experimentation motivated by the desire to gain the nutritional benefits of eating seaweed—nature's vegetables from the ocean. We eat it regularly as a main dish.'

KELP CHICKEN DELIGHT   Serves 2

2 tablespoons olive oil
1 onion, diced
1 head garlic, peeled and sliced
¾ cup minced fresh storm-cast bull kelp
¼ teaspoon salt
2 cups water
1 tablespoon vinegar
2 tablespoons soy sauce
¾ tablespoon chicken stock powder
2 bay leaves
pinch curry powder
small pinch pepper (or spices of your choice)
2 cups cooked diced boneless chicken
1 egg
½ cup grated tasty cheese
¼ cup chopped spring onions

Heat oil in frypan, add onion and garlic and cook gently until transparent. Add the kelp and salt and stir while heating. The colour of the kelp will change from brown to bright green. Continue stirring. The cooking mass will develop long sticky strands that adhere to the spoon when it is lifted from the pot.

Continue stirring while adding the water, vinegar, soy sauce, stock powder, bay leaves and spices. Heat until the liquid is reduced to a point where it has almost evaporated, stirring occasionally for approximately 20–30 minutes.

Add the chicken and stir through until warm. Remove bay leaves. Finally add the egg, cheese and spring onions, and stir through until the egg is cooked.

Dennis and Peta Klumpp, (below) King Island Produce, King Island

This dish features prime baby salmon from Ziggy Puka (right), a nearby fish grower at 41 Degrees South.

BABY SALMON & SILVER BEET   Serves 4

3 hot-smoked 41 Degrees South baby salmon

2 onions, very finely chopped

2 tablespoons virgin olive oil

pinch of ground star anise

salt and pepper

50ml (2½ tablespoons) raspberry vinegar

1 litre good red wine

1kg silver beet, washed and trimmed to green leaves only, stems discarded

50gm speck or bacon, chopped finely

2 garlic cloves, chopped

1kg pink-eye potatoes, cooked

200g good butter, cut in cubes

bunch of tarragon

Skin, clean and de-bone the salmon. Cover with cling-film and reserve. Place onions in a pan with olive oil, star anise, salt and pepper and cook gently until translucent. Add raspberry vinegar to the pan, let reduce, then add the red wine and reduce to a quarter the quantity. Cook silver beet in boiling water for 3 minutes then strain and refresh in cool water and strain again.

Gently fry the speck, add garlic, then silver beet, salt and pepper and a bit more olive oil, and cook over low heat for 15 minutes. Peel the potatoes, slice and cover with cling film and reserve.

To serve, place silver beet on a warmed serving dish. Lay the salmon on it and arrange sliced potato around the dish. Strain the sauce, then add butter until it reaches the right consistency. Season with salt and pepper and pour over the potatoes. Garnish with tarragon.

Remi and Ginette Bancal, Peppers Calstock, Deloraine

MUSHROOM & PEA LASAGNE   Serves 4

100g flour
1 egg
1 tablespoon of olive oil
600g fresh peas, shelled
100g dried mushrooms
500g whole fresh button mushrooms
50ml of fresh cream
salt and pepper to taste
3 tablespoons whipped cream

In the morning, or six hours beforehand, blend first three ingredients in a food processor until they make a dough that is shiny and does not stick.

Bring 2 litres of salted water to the boil, then add peas and cook for 5–7 minutes. Strain and mash them and put aside in a warm place.

Soak dried mushrooms in lukewarm water for 10 minutes and add fresh mushrooms, cooking for 15 minutes. Strain the mushrooms and reserve, then boil the liquid to reduce to a third. Chop mushrooms very finely. Put fresh cream in a pan, and season to taste with salt and pepper, add mushrooms and cook until thickened.

Roll dough out into small sheets and cook in boiling water for 1–2 minutes to make lasagne sheets. Drain, then assemble the lasagne. Put a little olive oil in the base of a baking dish, then a layer of lasagne sheets, the mushroom mixture, another layer lasagne, the pea puree, then lasagne again.

Bring the reserved mushroom juice to the boil, add whipped cream and season to taste before pouring over the lasagne and serving immediately.

Remi and Ginette Bancal, Peppers Calstock, Deloraine

This recipe was created by Andre Kropp, executive chef at the Henry Jones Art Hotel in Hobart. Anne Ashbolt suggests that the elderflower concentrate produced at her farm is 'great over fish as well as fruit and ice-cream.'

ROLLED ATLANTIC SALMON with DU PUY LENTILS & ASHBOLT ELDERFLOWER EMULSION

Serves 4

1 side of Dover Atlantic salmon
1 bunch coriander, chopped roughly
small knob of ginger, sliced
1 tablespoon palm sugar
zest of 1 lime
cracked black pepper

Ask your fishmonger to pin-bone and skin the salmon. Using a mortar and pestle make a paste from the coriander leaves, stalks, ginger, palm sugar and lime zest then season with black pepper. Place two layers of cling wrap (wider than the salmon) on the bench and place the salmon belly-side towards you on the front of the cling wrap. Using a meat mallet flatten the belly side to about 1.5 cm thick and spread on paste. Use the cling wrap to roll the salmon over itself to form a cylinder, then tie both ends to keep the roll tight. Place the roll in the freezer until starting to harden, trim ends square and cut into four equal portions, leaving the cling wrap on. Store in the fridge until needed.

To serve, pre-heat oven to 220°C. Leaving the cling wrap on, season the salmon's cut sides and sear cut sides only in a hot pan. When both sides are golden brown, place in oven for about 5 minutes or until the salmon is cooked to medium rare. Remove cling wrap.

Place a small mound of Du Puy Lentils (recipe follows) in the centre of each plate and drizzle Elderflower Emulsion dressing (recipe follows) around the mound. Place the salmon seared side up in the centre of the lentils. Top with a spoonful of Fig Chutney (recipe follows) and place a potato wafer standing on end, stuck into the chutney. Garnish with three sprigs of chervil or dill around each plate and serve.

ASHBOLT ELDERFLOWER EMULSION

2 tablespoons whole grain mustard
3 tablespoons Ashbolt elderflower concentrate
1 tablespoon red wine vinegar
6 tablespoons Ashbolt extra virgin olive oil
sea salt and cracked black pepper

Use a stick blender to combine mustard, elderflower concentrate and vinegar. While mixing slowly drizzle in the olive oil until emulsified. Season with salt and pepper.

DU PUY LENTILS

6 tablespoons butter
1 large onion, finely diced
1 garlic clove, minced
1 cup du puy lentils
3 cups chicken stock
1 carrot, finely diced
1 leek, finely diced
1 stick celery, finely diced
1 tablespoon red wine vinegar

Heat three tablespoons of the butter in a large saucepan and sweat the onion and garlic over a medium heat. When tender add the lentils and stir to coat them in the butter and onion. Add half the chicken stock and slowly bring up to the boil making sure they don't stick.

Check the lentils when the stock is almost absorbed and, if not cooked, continue adding small amounts of stock over a low heat and testing the lentils until they are tender. Do not overcook the lentils or they will break and go mushy. Fold carrot, leek and celery through the lentils, along with the remaining butter and red wine vinegar. Season to taste.

FIG CHUTNEY

1 small onion, diced
1 knob ginger, peeled and grated
8 dried figs, cut in pieces, hard stem removed
4 tablespoons white wine vinegar
$\frac{1}{2}$ cup water
$\frac{1}{2}$ cup castor sugar
1 tablespoon whole grain mustard
$\frac{1}{2}$ cup of toasted flaked almonds

Place onion, ginger, figs, vinegar, water, sugar and mustard in a small pot and simmer until the figs have broken down and the liquid has become syrupy, then fold through the almonds.

Anne Ashbolt, Ashbolt Farm, Plenty

This recipe is supplied by Red Ochre Restaurant, Adelaide, using possums are available from Lenah Game and Gourmet.

SWEET SPICED POSSUM BRAISE   Serves 16–20

4 whole possums
olive oil
rendered duck fat
1.5kg (6 cups) castor sugar
500ml (2 cups) water
175ml soya sauce
360ml fish sauce
extra 360ml (about 1½ cups) water
250g soya chilli paste
50g sambal oelek
(Available from Asian grocers)

Heat oven to 150°C. Cut the possum into small joints. Sear in a little olive oil. Place possum into a deep baking dish and add enough duck fat to just cover. Simmer slowly in duck fat for 4–5 hours until meat almost falls off the bone. Allow to cool, then strain and remove all meat. Dice meat. Bring the sugar and 500ml of water to the boil and cook to a golden caramel. Immediately add soya sauce, fish sauce, extra water and possum meat. Stir well. Add soya chilli paste and sambal oelek and simmer for 10 minutes.

Serve with Asian greens.

John Kelly & Katrina McKay,
Lenah Game and Gourmet, Mowbray

This delicious recipe combines cherry vinegar, dried sour cherries and Thornlea Cherry Liqueur.

SMOKED QUAIL OR CHICKEN with
SAVOURY CHERRY SAUCE   Serves 4

50g Ruby Lips dried sour cherries
(Available from gourmet outlets and some supermarkets)
1 cup Thornlea Cherry Liqueur
1 teaspoon brown sugar
1½ tablespoons cherry vinegar
(or red wine vinegar)
4 smoked quail, butterflied or
4 boned chicken thighs
oil or butter to fry

Soak the cherries in the liqueur for at least 30 mins. Combine all sauce ingredients in a small pan. Simmer for around 30 minutes or until the mixture becomes syrupy. Pan fry the quail or chicken in a little light oil or butter. The quail may be halved (or slice the chicken thigh) and arrange on a warm serving plate and serve with the sauce.

Elaine and Bob Hardy, Thornlea Wines, Sorell Fruit Farm, Sorell

This recipe was supplied by Relish Cooking School in Hobart, using wallabies available from Lenah Game and Gourmet Meats.

WALLABY STIR FRY   Serves 4

1 packet pepperberry wallaby, or small porterhouse steak
1 tablespoon fish sauce
1 teaspoon white sugar
4 tablespoons peanut oil
12 fresh basil leaves, shredded
1 large red chilli, finely sliced
3cm knob ginger, finely grated
2 garlic cloves, crushed
1 spring onion, finely sliced
juice of 1 lemon
salt and pepper
250g Hokkien or Singapore noodles, prepared as per packet instructions
extra basil leaves to garnish

Marinate the sliced wallaby in fish sauce and sugar for 15 minutes. Heat 1 tablespoon peanut oil in wok. Add shredded basil leaves and toss until crisp. Remove and drain on paper towel. Heat remaining oil in wok. Add chilli, ginger, garlic and spring onion. Cook for 30 seconds, tossing repeatedly. Add wallaby and cook quickly. Add fried basil and lemon juice, toss to combine, season to taste and serve piping hot over noodles, garnish with extra basil leaves.

PERFECT PAN-FRIED WALLABY

After opening the pack, allow the meat to 'breathe' for 5 minutes, just like a good red wine. If you prefer your meat cooked more on the medium side of rare, it is recommended that you marinate the wallaby in olive oil. This is not essential.

Pre heat the pan and add some olive oil. The oil will help the meat brown and retain its natural juices. Seal the juices in the meat by turning the cut immediately after placing in the pan until all sides are lightly 'browned'. Then allow 2–3 minutes cooking on each side. Remove from the pan and stand in a warm place for 5–10 minutes to rest prior to slicing.

Be careful to leave lots of space around each piece of wallaby when pan-frying. If the pan is overfilled the meat will stew in its juices producing a rather unsatisfactory result. Most importantly, the meat should be sliced across the grain (at 90 degrees) rather than along or diagonally across the grain. The way you slice meat to serve makes a huge difference to its eating quality.

John Kelly and Katrina McKay,
Lenah Game and Gourmet, Mowbray

This recipe was supplied by Paul Herbig, Drysdale Institute of TAFE, Launceston, using wallaby meat available from Lenah Game and Gourmet.

TART OF BRAISED WALLABY SHANKS with ONION & GOAT CHEESE SOUFFLÉ
Serves 4

sea salt and freshly ground white pepper

1 teaspoon coriander seeds

2 star anise

1 teaspoon fresh rosemary

1 teaspoon fresh oregano

6 garlic cloves

4 wallaby shanks

olive oil to fry

1 large carrot, diced

3 celery sticks, diced

1 medium onion, chopped

1 leek, sliced

3 cinnamon quills

grated zest of 1 orange and 1 lemon

3 tablespoons balsamic vinegar

170ml dry white wine

1 litre reduced brown veal stock

4 shortcrust pastry tart shells

Using a mortar and pestle crush the sea salt, pepper, coriander seeds, star anise, herbs and 1 garlic clove. Rub the mix over the wallaby shanks. Set aside. Heat some olive oil and saute the carrot, celery, onion and leek until lightly browned. Remove from pan and set aside. Seal shanks in the same pan, brown on all sides and remove.

Return vegetables to the pan along with cinnamon quills, orange and lemon zest and remaining garlic cloves. Brown until quite dark (not burnt) and deglaze with balsamic vinegar and white wine, scraping any sediment from the bottom. Place the vegetable base in the bottom of a braising pan and lay shanks on top. Cover completely with veal stock and cook slowly (at 150°C) for about 2–3 hours or until tender. When meat is 'falling off the bone', remove and set aside until cool. Strain the cooking juices, skim and reduce by half. Set aside for sauce.

To assemble and serve dish, using your fingers, shred wallaby meat from the bone and mix with a little Sauce Arabica (recipe follows) to bind. In the bottom of each of four cooked shortcrust tart shells place a good spoonful of onion compote (recipe follows), top with wallaby and chill. Make up a soufflé mix (recipe follows) and top each tart with this, bake 5 minutes in a preheated 180°C oven. Place cooked tart and soufflé on a spoonful of Sweet Potato Mash (recipe follows). Surround with Sauce Arabica and serve at once.

ONION COMPOTE

100g butter

100g Kaiserfleisch or bacon, julienned

6 onions, thinly sliced

2½ tablespoons honey

2½ tablespoons sherry vinegar

Melt butter in heavy-based saucepan, add bacon and onion and cook, covered, for 5 minutes or until onions start to wilt. Remove the lid and reduce to a simmer for about 3 hours, stirring regularly to prevent sticking. Remove from heat, stir in honey and vinegar and season to taste.

GOAT CHEESE SOUFFLÉ

60g butter
60g plain flour
350ml warm milk
75g goat cheese
1 tablespoon chopped fresh herbs
(parsley, chives, chervil)
1 tablespoon grated fresh parmesan
3 egg yolks
salt and pepper
4 egg whites

Melt butter in saucepan and add flour, cook for one minute, then cool slightly. Add milk, stirring all the while to form a sauce. Bring to the boil, reduce heat and simmer for 5 minutes. Mash goats cheese and add to sauce with chopped herbs and Parmesan. Allow to cool slightly. Fold in egg yolks and add seasoning to taste. Beat egg whites with a pinch of salt until creamy. Fold quickly into cheese mixture. Additional mix may be used for souffles.

SWEET POTATO MASH

200g sweet potato, cut into large even pieces
1 tablespoon olive oil
pinch sea salt
pinch nutmeg
50g soft butter

Roast peeled sweet potato with olive oil and sea salt until nicely coloured and cooked through. Drain off the oil and puree mixture in a food processor with nutmeg and butter. Set aside.

SAUCE ARABICA

1 onion, finely diced
1 carrot, finely diced
1 stick celery, finely diced
1 leek, finely diced
olive oil to fry
1 bay leaf
2 sprigs thyme
1 head garlic, halved across
1.5 litres braising liquor from wallaby
1.5 litres veal jus
1 cup crushed Arabica coffee beans
juice of 1 lemon
100g butter, cold, diced

Saute the vegetables in a little olive oil in a large frypan until dark. Add the herbs and garlic. Pour the braising liquor and veal jus over, bring to boil and simmer for 1½ hours. Strain, reduce by half and add coffee beans and infuse 1 hour. Strain again, add lemon juice and butter cubes just before serving.

NOTE: This will make at least 1 litre of sauce—more than needed for the recipe. If you wish to freeze it, leave out the butter until serving time.

John Kelly & Katrina McKay,
Lenah Game and Gourmet, Mowbray

BRAISED LAMB SHANKS with QUINCES FROM THE NEIGHBOUR, POMEGRANATE & CINNAMON   Serves 4

2 tablespoons olive oil
4 lamb shanks
salt and pepper
½ cup diced carrot
1 medium onion, diced
1–2 stalks celery, diced
1 head garlic, halved
5 bay leaves
10 cinnamon quills
5 cloves
10 juniper berries
200ml pinot noir
400ml beef stock
200ml demi-glace
(available from good delicatessans or providores)
20 baby carrots, sliced
20 baby leeks, sliced
100g clarified butter
2 quinces (peeled and cut into 20 even wedges and stored in water with lemon juice added)
2 tablespoons sangiovese verjuice
juice of half a pomegranate
20g butter
20 baby carrots, sliced
20 baby leeks, sliced
salt flakes
freshly ground pepper

Heat oil in a heavy-bottomed fry pan. Season and sear the lamb shanks, then add the carrot, onion, celery, garlic, bay leaves, five of the cinnamon quills, cloves, juniper berries wine and beef stock to a baking dish. Add the shanks to the baking dish, covering tightly with a double layer of foil. Put in a preheated 180°C oven for 1–2 hours. Half an hour before the shanks are ready, gently heat the demi-glace with the remaining five cinnamon quills and reduce to a glossy sauce consistency.

When the shanks are done, blanch the baby carrots and leeks and set aside. Heat a fry pan, add the clarified butter and the strained and dried quince wedges. Cook evenly and when you have an even golden colour, deglaze the pan with a splash of sangiovese verjuice and the pomegranate juice.

The verjuice and pomegranate juice will begin to evaporate. When it has almost cooked away, add the carrots and baby leeks along with butter and season to taste. Remove the shanks from the baking dish and arrange the carrot, leeks and quince wedges with shanks in the centre of the plate. Finish the dish with the demi-glace.

Richard Hooper, Pettavel Winery and Restaurant, Waurn Ponds

PEPPERED KING DORY

Serves 4

1 tablespoon fennel seed, roasted and ground

2 tablespoons white pepper, ground

500g king dory fillets, cleaned

250g saffron angel hair pasta
(Available at specialty delicatessens.)

¼ celeriac peeled, and cut in julienne

½ fennel bulb, finely sliced

½ tablespoons lemon juice

3 ½ tablespoons extra virgin olive oil

20 cherry tomatoes

1 garlic clove, finely sliced

olive oil

1 bunch continental parsley, cut finely

salt and pepper to taste

Mix fennel seed and pepper together and rub fish with this mixture. Cook pasta in boiling salted water until al dente, drain, then refresh, then drain again. Dress celeriac and fennel with lemon juice and some of the olive oil.

To serve, sear fish in a hot pan until cooked on both sides. Saute tomatoes and garlic in olive oil, add pasta and parsley and toss. Season to taste and place on plates with fish and celeriac salad on top.

Bernard McCarthy, Salix Restaurant, Willow Creek Winery, Merricks North

TIAN OF EGGPLANT

Serves 4

2 deboned quails

salt and pepper

1 ½ teaspoons ground lemon myrtle

2 large eggplants

oil for sauteeing

2 garlic cloves, crushed

1 small chilli, chopped

1 dessertspoonful white vinegar

100ml tomato puree

Vietnamese mint, chopped

virgin olive oil

extra Vietnamese mint leaves

Season quails with salt, pepper and ½ teaspoon of ground lemon myrtle, then cover and refrigerate overnight. Roast the eggplants in a 160°C oven. Carefully scoop out the flesh and mash roughly; reserve the eggplant skin. Put some olive oil, garlic, and chopped chilli in a hot pan for a minute then add eggplant, seasoning with salt, pepper, vinegar and the remaining teaspoon of ground lemon myrtle. Grill the quail, then cool.

Oil a gratin dish, arranging half the eggplant skin to cover the base of the dish, then layer the eggplant puree, sliced quail, and remaining eggplant puree, covering with the rest of the skin. Bake in a preheated 160°C oven for 30 minutes. Reheat the tomato sauce, season with salt, pepper, Vietnamese mint and virgin olive oil. Turn the tian onto a serving plate, pour sauce around it and decorate with mint leaves.

Remi and Ginette Bancal, Peppers Calstock, Deloraine

Marion Hansford and her husband Stewart Gilchrist love cooking with the wonderful regional produce available in this part of north-east Victoria. The potato gnocchi may be made the day before.

BRAISED LOCAL RABBIT GNOCCHI with
TOMATOES, CHORIZO, ROSEMARY & OLIVES   Serves 6

1 whole rabbit

game stock (substitute chicken stock if not available)

oil for frying

2 tablespoons chopped onion

200g chorizo sausage, cut into thin strips

2 garlic cloves, crushed

20 black olives, pitted

10 peeled and deseeded tomatoes, roughly chopped (tinned tomatoes may be substituted)

2 tablespoons freshly chopped rosemary

2 tablespoons chopped spring onions

30g butter

salt and pepper

1 teaspoon chopped parsley

freshly shaved parmesan

To braise the rabbit, preheat oven to 180°C. Place rabbit in a deep baking dish and add enough stock to cover. Braise for approximately 2 hours (actual time will vary depending on the size of the rabbit and the individual oven). Allow to cool in the dish. Once cool, remove the meat from the bone and cut into strips. Strain the remaining stock, then bring it to the boil in a saucepan and simmer until the stock has been reduced to approximately ⅓ litre. Set aside.

Heat olive oil in a large pan. Add onion and cook for 2 minutes. Add chorizo, then garlic and fry until beginning to brown. Season well. Add rabbit, olives and reduced stock. Cook for 3–4 minutes until warmed through. Add tomatoes, rosemary and spring onions. Cook for another 2–3 minutes. Stir through butter just before serving. Season to taste and serve in shallow bowls and sprinkle with parsley.

Arrange Potato Gnocchi (recipe follows) around the edge of each bowl. Serve with freshly shaved parmesan.

POTATO GNOCCHI

1–1½ kg baking potatoes,
to produce 800g cooked potato
150g parmesan cheese
scant cup plain flour
1 egg
2 egg yolks
salt and pepper
oil for frying
knob of butter

Bake whole potatoes in the oven until cooked. Scoop the flesh out from the skins and put through a potato ricer. If you don't have a ricer, mash thoroughly until there are no lumps.

Put the riced potato in a large mixing bowl and add the parmesan, flour, egg, egg yolks and seasoning. Mix well. Separate the dough into four equal amounts and wrap each in cling wrap. Roll each piece into a sausage shape approximately 2cm in diameter. Wrap in a second layer of cling wrap and secure tightly at each end, twisting the ends into the centre. Roll again making sure the package is of even shape and ensuring there are no air pockets and that it is watertight.

Poach these sausage-shaped packages in simmering water for approximately 10–12 minutes or until firm to the touch. When cooked, plunge the sausages into ice water and allow to cool. At serving time, remove gnocchi from the cling wrap and slice into 2–3cm thick slices.

Shallow fry in hot oil with a knob of butter for 2–3 minutes on each side until golden brown. Do not let the butter burn as this will taint and discolour the gnocchi. Do this in batches of no more than six at a time depending on the size of the frying pan and change the oil and butter after each batch.

Marion Hansford and Stewart Gilchrist
The Pickled Sisters Cafe, Wahgunyah

Celebrity chef Bart Beek of Essence Food Studio develops all the recipes for the Herb Barn. In this elegant dish, tender veal is flavoured with lemon tea tree and blue gum from Joes' Bush Billy Tea blend. The pungent yet creamy flavour from the blue cheese blends beautifully and will make this meal a memorable one.

BUSH TEA VEAL with
MUSHROOMS, GORGONZOLA & SPIRALI PASTA   Serves 4

2½ tablespoons Jingilli extra virgin olive oil

1 teaspoon The Herb Barn's Joes' Bush Billy Tea (use 1–2 teabags, or grind the loose leaf)

200g sliced tender veal fillet or back-strap

1 garlic clove, crushed

½ medium brown onion, finely chopped

10 small button mushrooms, cut in 2mm slices

1 cup thickened cream

2 tablespoons Gorgonzola or a rich blue vein cheese

300g Delverde spirali pasta or similar, cooked

4 tablespoons chopped walnuts

½ cup chopped continental parsley

seasoning to taste

In a heavy-based frying pan, add half the extra virgin olive oil and bring to moderate heat. Combine well the Bush Billy Tea and sliced veal. Add the veal to the pan and cook until well sealed, then remove and set aside. Add the remainder of the oil, heat up again then add the garlic. Cook for 10 seconds, and then add onion and mushrooms. When the mushrooms have turned light brown add the cooked veal, cream and Gorgonzola cheese. Blend well, then add the cooked pasta and walnuts. Lastly add the chopped flat leaf parsley, season to taste and serve immediately.

Serve with a mixed green salad and some good crusty bread.

Suzy Martin, The Herb Barn Pty Ltd, Tatong

JOES' BUSH BILLY TEA LAMB with ROESTI POTATOES and SPINACH

Serves 4

2 tablespoons The Herb Barn Joes'
Bush Billy Tea
1 garlic clove, crushed
1 x 5cm sprig rosemary, finely
chopped
teaspoon Tridosha native spice
2 tablespoons extra virgin olive oil
8 medium lamb fillets, trimmed of
sinew and fat
4 cups baby spinach
extra 2½ tablespoons extra virgin
olive oil
4 portions Roesti Potatoes
200ml lamb jus

Crush together in a mortar and pestle the tea, garlic, rosemary and native spice. Remove and place into a bowl together with the olive oil and lamb. Combine well and marinate for at least two hours in the refrigerator. Heat a grill pan and when very hot, cook the lamb to your desired rareness. Lightly saute the spinach in the extra oil.

Serve with crisp roesti (recipe follows), baby spinach and a little lamb jus.

ROESTI POTATOES

1kg potatoes
salt and pepper, to taste
3 tablespoons extra virgin olive oil
1 tablespoon butter

This wonderful Swiss classic can be made in various ways, plain or with the addition of onions and bacon. It is usually served to accompany meats, eggs or simply topped with melted cheese

Peel and steam the whole potatoes until half-cooked. When cool enough to handle, grate into a mixing bowl. Season well and gently fold through, being careful not to over mix the potato. Heat a heavy frypan and add half the olive oil and butter. Add the potato mix and gently pat down to form an even round shape in the pan.

Cook until golden, then place a large plate over the top and turn over. Place the frypan back onto the heat and add the remainder of the oil and butter. Now slide the roesti from the plate into the pan, cooked side up, and cook until the base is also golden. Slide onto a cutting board, cut into portions and serve immediately.

Suzy Martin, The Herb Barn, Tatong

JOES' BUSH BILLY TEA SWORDFISH with
MARINATED ZUCCHINI & FRESH TOMATO GLAZE   Serves 4

2 tablespoons The Herb Barn Bush Billy Tea
1 garlic clove
1 sprig rosemary, leaves only
2 tablespoons Mt Zero extra virgin olive oil
freshly cracked black pepper
sea salt flakes to taste
4 x 160g swordfish fillets, with skin on

Blend together tea leaves, garlic, rosemary, olive oil and seasoning. Coat swordfish fillets and set aside for 20 minutes. Grill on barbecue, skin side down until crisp, then turn and finish until just cooked. To serve, divide marinated zucchini (recipe follows) among four plates, place the tomato sauce (recipe follows) around the edges and top with grilled fish. Finish with a little drizzle of olive oil. Crisp Roesti Potatoes (see page 99) are delicious served with the swordfish.

MARINATED ZUCCHINI

2 medium zucchini, cut into long thin strips
½ bunch basil leaves, picked from stems and torn
1½ tablespoons white wine vinegar
2½ tablespoons Mt Zero olive oil (or any good quality extra virgin olive oil)
freshly cracked black pepper and sea salt flakes to taste

Place zucchini strips into a glass bowl with torn basil leaves, white wine vinegar, olive oil and seasoning. Leave to marinate while preparing other ingredients.

CLASSIC TOMATO SAUCE

8 ripe Roma (or egg) tomatoes, peeled, halved and seeded
⅓ cup Mt Zero olive oil (or any good quality extra virgin olive oil)
1 clove garlic, crushed
½ small onion, finely chopped
½ small celery stalk, finely chopped
6 torn basil leaves
¼ teaspoon sea salt flakes

Chop tomato flesh and put aside until needed. Warm the oil and cook the garlic for 20 seconds, then add the remainder of the ingredients and cook on medium for 10 minutes. Add tomatoes and simmer covered until the mixture is thick and glossy. Season well and blend in a processor until smooth. Reserve until required.

Suzy Martin, The Herb Barn, Tatong

In an unusual combination of ingredients, the snapper fillets are seasoned with The Herb Barn Citrus Twist tea, before being pan grilled and served with a black bean dressing.

SNAPPER FILLET with CITRUS TWIST CRUST

Serves 6

6 snapper fillets
6 teaspoons The Herb Barn Citrus Twist tea
½ teaspoon sansho pepper
1½ tablespoons Jingilli extra virgin olive oil
36 snow peas (trimmed and side strings removed)
2 cups cooked jasmine scented rice
6 tablespoons sambal goreng udang (Available from Asian stores)
⅓ cup chopped coriander leaves
2 tablespoons diced tomato

Make several cuts 1cm apart into the skin side of the snapper fillets. Rub in the Citrus Twist tea leaves and lightly sprinkle some of the sansho pepper on the skin side only. Refrigerate until required. Heat a heavy pan well, brush the snapper fillets with extra virgin olive oil and cook, skin side down. Hold the snapper down flat for 30 seconds—it will try to curl up otherwise. When crisp and golden, turn off the heat. Steam the snow peas for one minute and set aside.

To serve, place a serving of Jasmine Rice (see below) onto a warmed plate and pack down slightly. Top with the crispy sambel goreng udang, coriander, snow peas and the grilled snapper. Drizzle Black Bean Vinaigrette (recipe follows) over and sprinkle with a little diced tomato.

JASMINE RICE

3 parts unwashed jasmine rice
4 parts water

Place the jasmine rice and water into a suitably sized saucepan and bring to a rapid boil. Reduce heat to the lowest possible setting, cover with a lid and let cook for 10 minutes. Remove from the heat keeping the lid on firmly and let rest for at least 10 minutes. Loosen the rice grains with a fork and serve. Many flavour variations can be achieved by the addition of kaffir lime leaves, ginger, chilli etc.

BLACK BEAN VINAIGRETTE

2 tablespoons salted black beans (rinsed twice in cold water)
2 tablespoons peanut oil
2 tablespoons lime juice
2 tablespoons garlic, crushed
1 small green onion, finely sliced
1 tablespoon palm sugar

Combine all the ingredients in a blender and set aside.

Suzy Martin, The Herb Barn Pty Ltd, Tatong

Lakes Entrance, Victoria.

'The mountain pepper grows on our property,' says chef Darilyn Goldsmith, 'and I love creating interesting and complementary sauces. This suits the 'roo's natural sweetness. Overseas guests are intrigued by it.'

SEARED KANGAROO with
PEPPERBERRY SAUCE & WARRIGAL GREENS

Serves 4

MARINADE

4 tablespoons grapeseed oil
2 tablespoons ground mountain pepper leaf
8 torn mountain pepper leaves
2 teaspoons crushed mountain pepperberries
2 large garlic cloves, crushed

Mix all marinade ingredients together in a glass or chinaware dish and marinate kangaroo loins in it overnight.

SAUCE

1 cup reduced beef or veal stock
1 cup of red wine
2 tablespoons red currant jelly
½ cup of port

Prepare the sauce by combining the stock and wine with remaining marinade. Heat together and reduce by half then add red currant jelly and the port. Reduce until thickened and glossy.

4 kangaroo loins, trimmed of sinew
warrigal greens, blanched
knob of butter

Heat a heavy-based pan until smoking and sear kangaroo on both sides (it must remain rare) then remove and rest the meat.

Serve accompanied by sauce and warrigal greens which have been reheated with butter.

Les & Darilyn Goldsmith, Goldsmith's in the Forest,
Lakes Entrance

'This is my favourite way of cooking a pheasant breast fillet,' says Ros O'Bryan. 'Not just because the skin is deliciously crisp and the flesh, tender and succulent—but it is so versatile and can be served with so many different accompaniments and can even cooked on the barbecue. It is great when entertaining as almost everything can be done the day before.' You could substitute lentils, couscous or mashed potato for the barley risotto.

CRISPY SKINNED PHEASANT BREAST with TOASTED BARLEY RISOTTO & ROAST CARROT SAUCE

Serves 4

4 pheasant breast fillets
1 tablespoon olive oil
1 tablespoon butter

SPICE RUB

1½ tablespoons sea salt
1 teaspoon black peppercorns
6 juniper berries
¼ cinnamon stick
½ bay leaf
2 cloves
sprig of fresh thyme
sprig of fresh sage

Make the Spice Rub (mix together in a pestle and mortar ingredients listed).

Remove flesh from breast bone and rub one level teaspoon of Spice Rub into the skin only of each fillet. Heat butter and oil in a heavy based pan until butter is foaming. Add breast fillets, skin side down. Fry skin side at a steady sizzle for 5–8 minutes, depending on the size of the fillet, for example cook a 175g fillet for 6 minutes. Do not turn fillets during this time.

Lower heat, turn and cook underside at a very gentle sizzle and for 1½–3 minutes, again, time depends on the size of the fillet. Remove from pan and leave to rest in a warm place for 6–7 minutes. During this resting period the fillet will continue to cook slightly. It should be just faintly pink when served. Using a very sharp knife, slice fillet at an acute angle 2cm thick.

To serve, spoon Roast Carrot sauce (recipe follows) onto warmed serving plate. Place Risotto (recipe follows) in middle—a poly tube mould is good for this—then green vegetable across Risotto and lastly, carefully place sliced pheasant breast on top.

Serve with the same wine used in the risotto.

ROAST CARROT SAUCE

¼ cup extra virgin olive oil
2 cups chopped carrots (try organic carrots, you'll appreciate the difference)
2 garlic cloves, crushed
2 cups good chicken or pheasant stock
¼ cup white balsamic vinegar (optional)
salt and freshly ground pepper

Heat oil in a heavy-based pan, add the carrots and cook until slightly darkened and caramelised. Heat may need lowering to prevent carrots from burning. Add the garlic and cook briefly. Add the stock and vinegar, simmer gently to soften carrots. When tender, process sauce in blender until smooth. Taste and adjust seasoning. Reheat when ready to serve.

TOASTED BARLEY RISOTTO

1 cup pearl barley
2 tablespoons extra virgin olive oil
2 cups chopped onion
2 garlic cloves, crushed
1 cup red wine (shiraz, merlot or durif)
2–3 cups good chicken or pheasant stock
1 cup finely diced carrot
salt
freshly ground pepper
1 cup finely chopped chives

Place barley in large heavy-based frying pan, over a high flame. Shake pan to toast evenly all over until it is deep golden brown. Remove from pan. Heat olive oil in pan and fry onion gently until just starting to colour. Add garlic, cooking briefly. Add wine and reduce heat to medium. As the wine evaporates, add the barley and stir. Reduce heat to a simmer and begin adding stock gradually. Stir frequently, adding more stock as it is absorbed by the barley. Taste barley to see if it is cooked. It should not be soft, but retain a good texture. Add the carrots and continue to cook for a few more minutes. Season to taste. Add chives just before serving.

Ros O'Bryan, Olson Game Birds, Swan Hill

Brad Lobb describes this dish as a regionally specific, modern version of a French classic dish. 'It is a recipe I have been cooking and developing at home with my family and is about to be included in our seasonal menu,' he says. 'Allow plenty of cooking time. The dish may be prepared the day before. It was inspired by the regional produce of the Macedon Ranges and the culture of Slow Food in Australia and my own Spanish heritage.'

MACEDON RANGES REGIONAL RABBIT & PORK CASSOULET

Serves 8

300g dried white haricot beans, soaked in cold water overnight
1 onion, studded with a few cloves
1 bouquet garni (2 bay leaves, a few sprigs each of thyme and flat leaf parsley, tied together)
4 garlic cloves, peeled and finely chopped
black pepper
2 farmed or local wild rabbits, each cut into 4 pieces, brushed with olive oil
350g smoked Istra pork belly, cut into chunks
2 tablespoons Kyneton olive oil
1 large brown onion, chopped roughly
1 large carrot, chopped roughly
2 celery sticks, chopped roughly
350g Fernleigh Farm organic pork, diced
400g can tomatoes, chopped
1 tablespoon tomato purée
290ml Hanging Rock white wine
salt and pepper, to taste
2 heaped tablespoons fresh flat leaf parsley, chopped
1 heaped tablespoons fresh thyme, chopped
4 Istra fresh chorizo sausages, sliced thickly on the diagonal

Drain and rinse the beans, tip into a large pan and cover with cold water. Bring to the boil and skim as needed, then add onion, bouquet garni, two cloves of garlic and black pepper, as desired. Stir, and boil for 30 minutes more. Stir occasionally and top up with water when necessary. Preheat oven to 220°C. Season rabbit and place on a rack in a roasting tin. Roast for 15 minutes to seal, then remove and set aside. Lower oven heat to 140°C.

When the beans have been cooking for one hour, tip them into a sieve, discard the onion and bouquet garni. Put the pork belly in a flameproof dish and heat gently until the fat runs, then increase the heat and fry until just crispy. Add the olive oil and heat until sizzling, then add the onion, carrot, celery and remaining garlic. Fry over a gentle heat, stirring often, for 10 minutes. Use a slotted spoon to transfer to a plate. Increase the heat and add the diced pork and fry until coloured on all sides, then tip the ingredients from the plate back into the dish. Add the tomatoes, tomato purée, white wine and herbs, then season with salt and pepper to taste. Add haricot beans and 850ml water to the dish and bring to the boil. Stir, then lower the heat so the liquid is just simmering.

Keep the mixture in the same dish to cook or transfer it to an earthenware dish. Place the rabbit into the liquid, and add chorizo. Cover the dish with foil and bake for one hour, stirring once. Continue to cook uncovered for a further 1–1½ hours, stirring after 45 minutes, until the rabbit is really tender and the sauce is thickened. Take the dish out of the oven and remove the rabbit. Strip the meat from the bones and return the meat to the dish. Stir and add a little water, if necessary.

Brad Lobb

Return dish to the oven and bake for another 15 minutes until the meat and beans are very tender. Give the cassoulet a good stir. The consistency should be quite thick, if you prefer it slightly runnier, add a little water. Add parsley and thyme and adjust seasoning if necessary, then sprinkle the topping mixture (see below) over the surface in a thick even layer. Serve in warm bowls or small cassoulet dishes.

TOPPING

1 day-old loaf of ciabatta
2 garlic cloves, halved
4 tablespoons butter
2 heaped tablespoons chopped fresh flat leaf parsley
1 heaped tablespoon chopped fresh thyme

Tear the bread into pieces and put in a food processor. Add garlic and chop into coarse crumbs. Heat butter in a large frying pan until sizzling, then fry the breadcrumbs and garlic over a moderate to high heat for 5 minutes or until golden. Remove from the heat, toss in the herbs then season well with salt and pepper.

Brad Lobb, Campaspe Country House , Woodend

'The beauty of this dish is it is light and fresh, bringing out the sweetness of the crab,' says Nigel Harvey (far right). 'I cook this dish personally all the time and it can be substituted with prawns. It was one of our most popular on our autumn menu.'

PAPPARDELLE PASTA with BLUE SWIMMER CRAB, LILLIPUT CAPERS, SALSA VERDE & ROMA TOMATO Serves 4

500g pappardelle pasta
(or 8 lasagne sheets)
olive oil
200g fresh raw blue swimmer crab meat
3 garlic cloves, finely sliced
4 tablespoons white wine
2 red long chillies, deseeded and finely chopped
2 handfuls rocket leaves
50g lilliput capers (very small capers) or 2 tablespoons regular capers, rinsed
3 eschallots, finely sliced
2½ tablespoons extra virgin olive oil
juice of 2 lemons
4 Roma tomatoes, quartered, deseeded and chopped in small dice
handful of thinly sliced good quality parmesan

Bring a large pot of salted water to the boil and add a few drops of oil. Add pasta to boiling water and cook until al dente. Meanwhile place a large frying pan over high heat and add a little olive oil. When oil starts to smoke, toss in crab meat and a little of the garlic. Shake pan to colour all crab meat, add white wine and cook until crab changes from transparent colour. Take pan off the heat. Have a large bowl standing by with chilli, remaining garlic, rocket, lilliput capers, shallots and salsa verde (recipe follows). Drain the cooked pasta, add to bowl with the olive oil and lemon juice, give it a good toss and season to taste.

Serve immediately. Try to fold the pappardelle over, alternating the crab mix to give it a stack formation. Garnish with diced tomato and parmesan.

SALSA VERDE

half bunch basil
half bunch flat leaf parsley
2 garlic cloves
2–3 tablespoons salted capers, rinsed
2 anchovy fillets in oil, patted dry
2 tablespoons red wine vinegar
4 tablespoons extra virgin olive oil
2 teaspoons Dijon mustard
sea salt and black pepper to taste

Finely chop herbs, garlic, capers, and anchovy fillets and place in a bowl. Drizzle in red wine vinegar whisking well and slowly adding oil. Mix in mustard, season to taste, and refrigerate until needed.

Nigel Harvey, Voyager Estate Winery, Margaret River

Accompaniments

Fetabelle is a triple Gold Medal-winning feta-style cheese. 'This recipe was such a hit in the Hunter Belle Cheese test kitchen (my mother-in-law Liz), that when left alone my husband and father-in-law made extra batches for themselves! Simple and very yummy.'

FETABELLE SALSA   Serves 2–3

200g Fetabelle, crumbled
1 Spanish onion, roughly
chopped
2–3 tablespoons olive oil
4 medium tomatoes, seeded and
chopped
2 tablespoons sweet chilli sauce
chopped coriander and basil
leaves
cracked black pepper, to taste

Toss all ingredients together and serve on toasted ciabatta bread.

Kate Woodward, Hunter Belle Cheese, Muswellbrook

A tasty, low cholesterol vegetable dish—if served without the toppings! You can substitute sweet potatoes if desired.

'SIMPLE' SQUASHED POTATOES   Serves 4–6

6 medium potatoes, washed but
unpeeled
rock or flavoured salt, optional
1 tablespoon Simply Green Tomatoes
olive oil

Cook potatoes until soft by boiling, steaming or micro-waving. If desired, add a little rock salt, or flavoured salt before cooking. Place the potatoes between sheets of paper towelling and squash to flatten them slightly. Place them on an oven tray and cover the potatoes with Simply Green Tomatoes and oil. Bake in a moderate oven until nicely browned.

A tasty, low cholesterol vegetable dish—if served without the toppings! You can substitute sweet potatoes if desired.

'SIMPLE' OVEN BAKED POTATOES   Serves 4-6

6 medium potatoes, peeled and thinly sliced

4 tablespoons Simply Green Tomatoes (drained)

(Reserved oil can be used for pan frying chicken, fish or steak or salad dressings.)

Mix the potatoes and Simply Green Tomatoes together and place in a baking dish. Bake in moderate oven for 20-30 minutes. If desired, add favourite toppings, such as grated cheese, chopped bacon and/or breadcrumbs) before cooking.

This is a 'fantastic crowd pleaser'.

'SIMPLE' SURPRISE PUMPKIN   Serves 6-8

1 small whole pumpkin

2 tablespoons Simply Green Tomatoes

1 medium brown onion, finely sliced

3 rashers of bacon, diced finely

3 cups seasoned breadcrumbs

2 cups grated tasty cheese

1 cup cream

2 tablespoons roasted pine nuts

Wash pumpkin, cut a small circle in the top for the lid. Scoop out the seeds and stringy flesh and discard. Place the pumpkin aside for filling. Combine Simply Green Tomatoes, onion and bacon in a frypan and stir together over a low heat for 3 minutes. Add remaining ingredients and mix well. Fill this mixture into the cavity of the pumpkin, replace lid and bake in slow to moderate oven for approximately 2 hours or until soft to touch.

Keep the lid on until ready to serve. Remove lid and scoop a little flesh and stuffing together onto plates.

Marilyn Lanyon , Simply Tomatoes, Boort, Victoria

Desserts

Quinces are grown locally and the following recipe was developed, Mark says, 'from experimenting with different regional ingredients and home-grown fruits to create a delicious comfort food cake'.

QUINCE CAKE   Serves 8–10

1¼ cups castor sugar
2½ cups water
4 quinces, peeled, quartered and cored
1 vanilla bean, split lengthways
200g soft unsalted butter
200g castor sugar
4 eggs
1 teaspoon vanilla extract
1¼ cups self raising flour, sifted
80g ground almonds
140ml Greek-style yoghurt
icing sugar and whipped cream, to serve

Combine sugar and water in a saucepan, stirring over a low heat until sugar dissolves. Bring to the boil, then remove from heat. Place quince quarters and vanilla bean in a heavy-based roasting pan, pour the sugar syrup over, cover with foil and bake at 150°C for 2–2½ hours or until quince is tender.

Remove foil and cool quince in syrup. Drain quince, reserving syrup, and slice each piece lengthways into thirds. In a bowl, beat butter and sugar until light and fluffy, then add eggs, one at a time, beating well after each addition. Add vanilla extract and beat for another minute, then fold in flour and ground almonds until just combined. Stir in yoghurt, then spoon half the batter into a lined 24cm springform pan and cover with half the poached quince quarters, slightly overlapping, then cover with remaining batter. Bake in a preheated 180°C oven for an hour or until a cake tester comes out clean.

Cover top of cake with baking paper if browning too quickly. Serve wedges of cake, warm or at room temperature, dusted with icing sugar, accompanied by cream and a few slices of reserved poached quince and a little poaching liquid to the side.

Mark and Annette Kern, Bush Rock Cafe, Blackheath

'When I first tried lemon myrtle, I thought it would partner very well with the velvety smoothness of the cheesecake and give a fresh zing to the sweetness,' says Jane Westcott, who makes it every week now for the cafe. She reminds cooks that for the best success with this recipe, the cream cheese must be beaten very well. The cheesecake is best made a day ahead, and will keep, refrigerated, up to a week.

PERENTI CAFE LEMON MYRTLE CHEESECAKE   Serves 12

250g plain biscuits (such as Nice), finely crumbed

125g melted butter

500g cream cheese, at room temperature

400g condensed milk

1 teaspoon vanilla essence

⅓ cup fresh lemon juice

1 tablespoon ground lemon myrtle

⅓ cup lemon curd or lemon butter, preferably home-made

1 extra teaspoon ground lemon myrtle

Mix biscuit crumbs and melted butter together and press onto the base and up the sides of a 24cm springform tin with a removable base. Refrigerate while making filling. Using a mixer, beat cream cheese on medium speed until smooth, around 7 minutes. Add condensed milk and beat again for another 5 minutes until velvety smooth. Stir in vanilla, lemon juice and lemon myrtle. Pour over base and refrigerate several hours until set. Make topping by heating lemon butter gently (use a microwave to do this) before pouring over cheesecake and spreading evenly. Sprinkle with extra lemon myrtle.

Jane Westcott, Perenti Cafe and Catering, Gloucester

Near Gloucester, North Coast, New South Wales.

AVOCADO ICE-CREAM   Serves 4

200g sugar
170ml dry white wine
120g liquid glucose
150ml water
4 ripe Hass avocados
juice of 2 lemons
150ml milk

In a small saucepan dissolve the sugar, white wine, glucose and water over a low heat, then set aside to cool. Transfer mixture to a food processor, add the avocados and lemon juice and puree until very smooth. Mix in the milk. Churn the mixture in an ice-cream machine until frozen and store in freezer. Set for at least 2 hours before serving.

BANANA TART TATIN with RUM & RAISIN ICE-CREAM

Serves 4

100g castor sugar
100g unsalted butter
2 tablespoon dark rum
4 large lady finger bananas
1 puff pastry sheet
4 dried vanilla bean fans
4 scoops rum and raisin ice-cream

Put sugar into a heavy-based saucepan and heat very gently until it melts. Add butter and allow to melt over a medium heat, shaking the pan to blend the butter with the sugar. Boil to a medium dark brown caramel, but do not allow it to burn. Immediately take off the heat and stir in the rum. Pour the caramel into 4 cast iron pans or tart tins and spread with the back of a spoon. Cool until set.

Peel each banana and slice diagonally into 5 to 6 pieces and place onto caramel in the pans. Cut out circles from puff pastry the same size as the pan and drape over the banana, tucking in edges. Rest in fridge for at least 30 minutes. Preheat oven to 200°C. When almost ready to serve, place the pans onto a heavy baking sheet and cook in the oven for 12–15 minutes until pastry is crisp and light golden brown. Leave to stand for 1 minute, then carefully flip tarts onto warmed plates. Trickle over some of the pan juices and serve each with a dried vanilla bean fan (see below) and ice-cream.

VANILLA BEAN FANS

Take a vanilla bean and, using a knife, cut it lengthways down the middle leaving it joined at one end. Scrape out seeds and reserve for use in ice cream. Split the two halves again down the middle still leaving end in tact. Carefully spread bean into a fan and place between two baking trays. Place into oven at 180°C and cook until room fills with the smell of vanilla. Take out of oven and remove top tray, let cool and carefully transfer to airtight container. Dust with icing sugar to serve. Great with coffee.

Kane Shaw, Flooded Gums Restaurant, Bonville International
Golf Resort, Bonville

'Comboyne blueberries, grown organically, need a 'support' and from the idea of a light dish, a mousse was born ... and now this is our award-winning dessert.'

COMBOYNE BLUEBERRIES FLAMBÉ tossed in BAGO VINEYARD WHITE PORT & served with MARROOK FARM YOGHURT LIME MOUSSE

Serves 4; if making quenelles, serves 6

130g Marrook Farm country style (or bush honey, wattle seed or lemon myrtle) yoghurt
130 g creme fraiche
juice of 1 lime
50g icing sugar
2 ½ leaves gelatin
130ml whipped cream
2 egg whites
1 tablespoon sugar

Mix yoghurt, creme fraiche and lime juice in a bowl, and add icing sugar. Soften gelatin in cold water, strain and mix through the yoghurt mixture, then add whipped cream and fold through. Beat egg whites and sugar until stiff and fold into the yoghurt mixture. Spoon into moulds, or a big bowl to later shape into quenelles. Put the mousse in the fridge to set.

To serve, unmould mousse onto dessert plates, or using two spoons, shape quenelles from the set mousse. Place on cold plates and spoon Flambéed Blueberries (recipe follows) around.

FLAMBÉED BLUEBERRIES

1 teaspoon butter
2 tablespoons brown sugar
3 punnets Comboyne blueberries
60ml Bago Vineyard white port

Melt butter in a pan, add brown sugar then blueberries, and toss until coated. Add port and flambé.

Wolfgang Zichy, The Moorings Restaurant & Cafe, Harrington

As this is a fairly rich recipe, you don't need much for each serve. Barbara Barlin usually makes it in a square tin and serves it in small squares with coffee.

LEMON MYRTLE CHEESECAKE OR SLICE
Serves 8–12

½ cup crushed macadamias
12 biscuits, either Arnotts Nice or
Milk Coffee (or mixed), finely crushed
125g butter, melted

Add crushed macadamias to biscuit crumbs, and mix in butter. Press firmly into pie plate or biscuit tray. Refrigerate until required.

CHEESECAKE FILLING
125g margarine or butter
250g cream cheese
¾ cup castor sugar
2 teaspoons vanilla essence
2 teaspoons ground lemon myrtle
2 teaspoons powdered gelatin
70ml hot water

Cream butter, cream cheese, sugar and vanilla essence. Add lemon myrtle. Dissolve gelatin in hot water, cool, then add gradually to mixture. Beat until fluffy. Pour mixture on top of biscuit base and spread evenly. Refrigerate before serving for about an hour.

To make a Lemon Myrtle Cheesecake Slice, instead of the base used above, use 2 packets Lattice biscuits to line a 25cm x 20cm (10 inch x 8 inch) tray with biscuits placed glossy side down. Pour Cheesecake Mixture on top and spread evenly. Place more biscuits on top, glossy side up. Refrigerate before serving. Great with Coffee.

Barbara Barlin, Barbushco, Lorne

'This recipe was given to me by a customer of mine, Tricia Duncombe. It is a favourite of many customers and so easy to make.'

MANDARIN, ALMOND & CHOCOLATE (FLOURLESS) CAKE

8 mandarins, unpeeled
12 eggs
500g castor sugar
1 tablespoon baking powder
500g almond meal
1 cup chopped dark couverture (cooking) chocolate

Place mandarins in a heavy-based saucepan, cover well with water and bring to the boil. Boil for about two hours, drain and set aside to cool. Grease and line a 28cm cake tin. Chop and seed mandarins and place in a food processor until smooth. Transfer to a large bowl and add eggs, sugar and baking powder. Fold in almond meal and chocolate. Bake in a preheated 180°C oven for approximately 1 hour or until firm to the touch. Serve with double cream and Candied Peel (recipe follows).

CANDIED PEEL

1 cup sugar
1 cup water
½ cup chopped mandarin or orange peel

Bring sugar and water to the boil. Boil for 5 minutes and add the peel. Boil for a further 20 minutes, then strain and pour over warm cake.

Donna Carrier, Bent on Food Regional Produce Store, Wingham

This recipe is part of the ever-changing menus at The Moorings restaurant, with a focus on fresh local organic produce from the Manning Valley and surrounding areas.

STRAWBERRY-RHUBARB UNDER MERINGUE GRATIN

Serves 2

4 stalks rhubarb
250g strawberries
2 tablespoons apple juice
4 tablespoons honey
3 egg whites
1½ tablespoons castor sugar

Wash and clean rhubarb and strawberries. Cut half the rhubarb stalks into small pieces. Add these to 100g strawberries and apple juice in a saucepan. Bring to the boil and add honey. Puree this mixture and press through a sieve. Cut and blanch the other two rhubarb stalks, and halve the remaining strawberries. Put aside until needed. Beat egg whites and sugar to a firm meringue consistency.

To serve, select 2 white heatproof plates, arrange the rhubarb and strawberries in the centre and top with puree. Spoon the Creme Anglaise (recipe follows) over the fruit and pipe meringue in a spiral over the top. Place under a grill until meringue sets and lightly browns. Serve immediately.

CREME ANGLAISE (VANILLA SAUCE)

1 vanilla pod
250ml cream
4 egg yolks
1½ tablespoons castor sugar
juice of a lemon

Split the vanilla pod and scrape out the seeds. Add both to the cream and bring to the boil. Whisk egg yolks and sugar to a frothy consistency, carefully add cream mixture, pod removed, and whisk mixture over a bowl of hot water until ribbon consistency. Add lemon juice to taste, cover with cling wrap and put aside.

Wolfgang Zichy, The Moorings Restaurant and Cafe, Harrington

For this recipe, the skin of black sapotes must have turned brown in colour, almost looking over-ripe. They'll be very 'squishy' but it is then that the pulp resembles chocolate pudding!

BLACK SAPOTE TORTE

Serves 12

270g butter
1½ cups castor sugar
6 eggs
2¼ cups self raising flour
¼ cup plain flour
¼ cup milk
2½ cups black sapote (chocolate pudding fruit) pulp
3 teaspoons bicarbonate of soda

Cream butter and sugar. Beat eggs and add very slowly to the creamed mixture. Mix well and stir in half the sifted flours, half the milk, half the sapote pulp, then repeat until all is used. Stir in bicarbonate of soda. Place mixture in three round, greased 25cm cake pans and bake in a preheated moderate oven for approximately 35–40 minutes until done. Remove from oven and cool on a rack. Spread each cake layer with frosting and poached tamarillos (recipes follow). Decorate top and sides of cake with remaining frosting and poached tamarillos.

BLACK SAPOTE FROSTING

250g unsalted butter
8 cups icing sugar
1 cup mashed sapote
1 teaspoon vanilla
¼ cup Kahlua

Cream butter and icing sugar until fluffy. Gradually add black sapote, vanilla and Kahlua.

POACHED TAMARILLOS

18 tamarillos
4 cups port
3 tablespoons cherry brandy
4 cloves
1 cinnamon stick
1 vanilla bean

Remove tamarillo skins, leaving stalks attached. Place in a saucepan with all other ingredients, simmer for 10 minutes and let cool in liquid. Remove stalks and slice 12 tamarillos to use in filling the cake, and use the remaining 6 sliced lengthways to decorate the top.

Sally Brinsmead, Tropical Fruit World, Duranbah

As in all Paul Benhaim's recipes, for this dessert you 'prepare' the food rather than cooking it.

NOT CHOCOLATE MERINGUE   Serves 2

1 avocado, skinned and de-seeded

½ –1 tablespoon hemp butter*

1 tablespoon carob powder, or 2 tablespoons cacao nibs (raw chocolate)

3 fresh dates, or 4 dried dates, soaked

½ tablespoon maple syrup

crushed hemp nut to garnish (Contact Alive Foods for suppliers)

thin ½ slice of lemon

Blend all ingredients thoroughly until smooth. Serve in a glass garnished with a thin half slice of lemon and sprinkle of hemp nut.

Paul Benhaim, Alive Foods, Montville

Although Ulli Spranz says she prefers natural vanilla essence, available from health food stores, you may substitute a packet of vanilla sugar, bought in small packets from supermarkets. Vanilla sugar may however vary in strength. Experiment a little until you find the brand and amount you like.

BLACK FOREST PIE   Serves 12

1 cup plain flour
3 tablespoons sugar
zest of ½ lemon
1 egg yolk
75g Swiss-style quark
40g cold butter
butter, for greasing

Put the flour into a bowl and add the sugar, lemon zest, egg yolk and quark. Cut the butter into pieces and add. Knead with your hands, quickly, until an even dough is achieved. If the dough is kneaded for too long it will become hard when being baked. Keep the dough cool for an hour. Grease a 26cm tray and roll dough out evenly to cover.

Spread onto dough in the pan and bake on the lowest rack in a preheated 220°C oven for 25 minutes. To serve, add Filling and Topping. Serve with freshly whipped cream.

FILLING
½ tablespoon milk
2 eggs
2 egg yolks
1 teaspoon vanilla essence
4 tablespoons sugar, depending on sweetness of fruit
450g Swiss-style quark
4 tablespoons cornflour

Make filling by mixing well the milk, eggs, egg yolk, vanilla essence, sugar, quark and half the cornflour.

TOPPING
500g berries (strawberries, blackberries, raspberries, black or red currants)
100g sugar, extra
2 tablespoons cornflour
3 tablespoons cold water

Heat the berries and add sugar. Mix the remaining 2 tablespoons of cornflour with water and add to the berries, stirring to combine. Boil until the liquid thickens slightly. Before serving, spread the berries evenly over the cake and allow to cool.

Ulli Spranz, B.-d. Farm Paris Creek, Meadows

The recipe for this delicious dessert arrived in the Cantrills' mail as a lovely, handwritten, anonymous note. The pudding is mentioned in A Legacy, *a novel of life in Berlin in the 1890s, and was eaten by rich Berliners before going to hear the famous Australian opera singer, Nellie Melba.*

NESSELRODE PUDDING

Makes 2 litres, Serves 16

250g fine chestnut puree (see below)
1 litre egg custard
125g each of crystallised cherries and candied orange peel, soaked overnight in muscat wine
125g each seedless raisins and currants, soaked in muscat, cassis or port
500 ml cream (King Island) whipped

Fold chestnut puree into custard, then add soaked fruits and finally the cream. Freeze in a mould. Unmould onto a serving plate and serve cut in wedges.

Deborah Cantrill, Nirvana Organic Produce, Heathfield

Dried chestnut pieces can be used in most recipes calling for fresh chestnuts. Cover them with water, bring to the boil, remove from heat and soak overnight. They can then be cooked as you would fresh peeled chestnuts. Generally, 250g dried chestnuts reconstitutes to approximately 700g fresh ones.

NIRVANA CHESTNUT ICE-CREAM

Serves 8

250g chestnut puree
1 litre ice-cream (home-made if possible)
300ml cream, whipped
500g mixed dried fruit, soaked overnight in Cassis or brandy

Mix chestnut puree (recipe below), ice-cream, cream and fruit together and re-freeze. When half-frozen, mix with a fork and re-freeze in a mould, or add ingredients to ice-cream machine.

CHESTNUT PUREE

600g fresh chestnuts, peeled (or dried chestnut, soaked)
milk, water or stock (water preferable)
sugar
salt

Put chestnuts in a saucepan, cover with liquid, and simmer gently until soft. Mash and put through a mouli, which makes the best quality puree, or blend in food processor. Add salt or sugar to taste. Use immediately or store in the fridge for 24 hours or freeze.

Deborah Cantrill, Nirvana Organic Produce, Heathfield

PEAR PUDDING

Serves 4

5 pears, peeled, halved and cored, then cut in pieces
juice and grated zest of 1 lemon
2 tablespoons sugar
500g German-Style (low fat) quark
½ cup sugar
2 tablespoons cinnamon
3 egg yolks
3 tablespoons hot water
4 tablespoons cornflour
1 tablespoon baking powder
4 tablespoons sultanas
4 egg whites
a little icing sugar

Marinate pears in lemon juice and 2 tablespoons sugar. Mix quark with ½ cup sugar, cinnamon, egg yolks, lemon zest and water until a creamy consistency. Sift in the cornflour and baking powder. Mix well. Add the sultanas and pears. Beat the egg whites until stiff and fold into the mixture. Place in a greased ovenproof dish and bake in a preheated 180°C oven for 30 minutes. Dust with icing sugar and serve hot.

Ulli Spranz, B.-d. Farm Paris Creek, Meadows

This tastes best after two days.

QUARK CHOCOLATE FLAN Serves 4-6

200g soft butter
50g cocoa
200g sugar
2 eggs
400g flour
1 tablespoon baking powder
butter, for greasing

Beat butter until it is light and creamy. Add cocoa and sugar and mix well. Add the eggs and stir until creamy, then add the flour and baking powder, mixing until smooth. Put this dough for the base in fridge to cool down for 2 hours.

Halve the dough and put one half back into the fridge. Halve dough again and spread the quarter piece onto a springform tray approximately 26–28cm using the other quarter to form the sides. Spread filling evenly over the base. Form 2cm balls out of the remaining dough and arrange over top of quark filling. Bake in a preheated 180°C oven for 70 minutes. Let cool and then remove the base of the springform tray.

FILLING

125g soft butter
150g sugar
3 x 50g packets vanilla sugar
4 tablespoons rum
3 egg yolks
30g cornflour
500g German-style
(low fat) quark cheese
300g Swiss-style quark cheese
3 egg whites

Beat butter until creamy. Add sugar, vanilla sugar, rum and egg yolks and stir until light and creamy. In a separate bowl, add cornflour to the quarks and mix well. Add to the filling mixture and mix well. Beat egg whites until stiff and fold in to the quark mixture.

Ulli Spranz, B.-d. Farm Paris Creek Pty. Ltd, Meadows

Jill Allanson suggests that you store a jar of sugar or icing sugar with some lavender seed in it for at least a week to allow the flavour to penetrate, then sieve and add to your favourite meringue recipe, using up those left-over egg whites.

HONEY & LAVENDER CREAM DESSERT   Serves 6

1 tablespoon English lavender (L.angustifolia) seed (Available from Lyndock Lavender Farm)
¼ cup boiling water
8 egg yolks, lightly beaten
¼ cup sugar
1 cup cream
¼ cup honey
1 cup cream, whipped
2 egg whites, stiffly beaten
honey and lavender for garnish

Sprinkle lavender seed on boiling water and allow to stand for 30 minutes. Strain and reserve liquid. Place egg yolks and sugar in bowl, beating until light and fluffy. Gradually add cream. Transfer to top of double saucepan and heat until thickened, stirring constantly. Do not allow mixture to boil. Remove from heat, add reserved liquid and honey. Allow to cool. When cool fold in whipped cream and egg whites. Pour mixture evenly into six individual serving dishes. Refrigerate overnight.

To serve, drizzle with honey and garnish with lavender head.

Jill Allanson, Lyndoch Lavender Farm & Cafe, Lyndoch

'My mother, Irma, remembers this as a dish her family ate only on Christmas Eve,' says Ingrid Glastonbury. 'My daughter Tullia made it for the café the first December we were open, and she found pounding of the poppy seeds in a mortar and pestle for 20 minutes quite exhausting!' However, do use the mortar and pestle when you make this dish, as a food processor doesn't work.

MOHNKLOESE ('POPPY SEED CLUMPS')   Serves 4

2 cups milk
5 tablespoons white sugar
250g ground poppy seeds
50g sultanas
5 tablespoons rum
50g almond slivers
1 teaspoon cinnamon
2 drops bitter almond oil, (or ground bitter almonds)
12–16 slices zwiebach (oven toasted bread) or white bread
almond flakes to garnish

Gently heat milk and add sugar. When dissolved reserve half of this mixture. Pour the other half over ground poppy seeds and leave to swell. Add sultanas, rum, almond slivers, cinnamon and bitter almond oil. This mixture is best left overnight for the flavours to combine. Soak bread briefly (it must not become mushy) in remaining milk. Layer the poppy seed mixture and the soaked bread in a bowl, finishing with the poppy seed mixture. Sprinkle with flaked almonds.

Ingrid Glastonbury, Krondorf Road Café, Kabminye Wines,
Krondorf

Elderflower concentrate from New Norfolk, local strawberries, Tasmania's own Tazziberries (myrtus berries) all sourced from co-operative farms from around Tasmania, make this a regional delight.

ELDERFLOWER SEMIFREDDO & APPLE TISANE
Serves 4

200ml pouring cream
½ teaspoon vanilla extract
3 eggs, separated
1¼ tablespoons castor sugar
2½ tablespoons Ashbolt elderflower concentrate syrup
diced fresh fruit

Whip cream and vanilla lightly. Cream egg yolks and sugar then fold in cream and elderflower syrup. Whisk whites into soft peaks and gently fold into mix, in three additions. Divide equally between rounded moulds (coffee cups will do) and freeze. Keep covered to stop crystals from forming. To serve, place diced fruit such as strawberries, kiwifruit, raspberries, oranges and tazziberries in serving dishes. Unmould semifreddo onto fruits and pour chilled tisane (recipe follows) over each dessert. Serve immediately.

APPLE TISANE
1 cup warm water
1 tablespoon Turkish apple tisane powder
(Available from T2 stores.)

Bring water to the boil. Stir in powder until completely dissolved. Chill overnight.

Justin Harris, Source Restaurant, Moorilla Estate, Berriedale

Best served with a glass of Sparkling Cuvee, such as 2001 Moorilla Estate Brut.

Semifreddo translates from Italian as 'semi-frozen'. Before serving, the dessert is partially softened which allows a greater intensity of flavour. This dessert doesn't require an ice-cream maker. 'To make it easier we have used good quality prepared custard,' say the Hardys, 'but of course you can make your own if you wish.' This dessert has the advantage of being able to be prepared in advance. When it is frozen, wrap it in cling wrap then over-wrap in aluminium foil, and it will keep well for several weeks.

BLACKCURRANT CHEESECAKE SEMIFREDDO   Serves 8

250g blackcurrants
150g castor sugar
2 tablespoons blackcurrant liqueur
500g mascarpone
300ml fresh custard, cooled
1 teaspoon vanilla essence
1 extra tablespoon blackcurrant liqueur
100g crunchy oat biscuits (such as Butternut Snaps), crushed finely
50g butter, melted

Line a 1kg loaf tin with baking paper to cover the base and the sides. Place blackcurrants in a small saucepan with half the sugar and the blackcurrant liqueur. Bring to the boil and then simmer for 5 minutes or until the fruit is softened. Push the blackcurrants through a sieve, being sure to press out as much of the pulp as possible. Divide the mixture into two equal parts and leave to cool. Add the extra tablespoon of liqueur to the second portion as this is used as a sauce. Lightly beat mascarpone until soft. Be careful not to over-beat as the mascarpone may separate.

Gradually fold in cold custard, remaining sugar and vanilla. Drizzle a little of the first portion of the blackcurrants over the base of the lined tin. Add half the mascarpone mix to the tin, then a little more of the blackcurrants. Add the rest of the mixture and then top with the remaining blackcurrants. Swirl the mixtures together with a skewer. Combine biscuit crumbs with the melted butter.

Smooth the top cheesecake mixture and sprinkle evenly with the crumb mixture, pressing lightly to consolidate them. Cover tightly with cling wrap and foil and freeze for at least four hours or overnight. Keep the remaining sauce refrigerated or freeze if you are not planning to use the dessert straightaway.

To serve, transfer the loaf tin to the refrigerator one hour before serving or until it has softened slightly. Turn semifreddo out of tin, carefully remove the lining paper, then turn onto a long flat serving tray so that the crumb topping is on top. Cut into slices and serve with the reserved sauce.

Elaine and Bob Hardy, Thornlea Wines, Sorell Fruit Farm, Sorell

The recipes from Sorell Fruit Farm were developed by Ms Judith Sweet who is a leading Tasmanian food writer and food critic. This cheesecake is of a light consistency achieved by combining cream cheese and ricotta. The glaze is full of flavour and colour. If you wish, you can top the cheesecake with lightly whipped and sweetened cream to replace the glaze.

CHEESECAKE with RASPBERRY LIQUEUR GLAZE   Serves 8

250g crunchy oat biscuits (such as Butternut Snaps), crushed
75g butter, melted
500g cream cheese, softened
250g ricotta
4 eggs
1 teaspoon vanilla essence
1½ cups fresh or frozen raspberries
2 tablespoons raspberry liqueur

Combine biscuit crumbs and butter and press very firmly into the base of a 23cm springform tin. Place the springform tin onto a baking tray. Cook in a preheated 150°C oven for around 20 minutes. In a large bowl combine the cheeses and add the eggs and vanilla. Beat with an electric hand-held mixer until the mixture is totally smooth.

Pour the mixture into the tin (still on the baking tray), scatter raspberries on top of the mixture then drizzle with the liqueur. Return to the oven and bake for a further 40 minutes, then turn heat off and leave the cheesecake in the oven until it is cool. Chill for at least 2 hours, preferably up to 8 hours. Make the glaze (recipe follows) shortly before serving, allowing time for it to cool and set.

Close to serving, spread the cooled glaze onto the chilled cheesecake and place back in the refrigerator for a few minutes until set. Serve with whipped cream or ice-cream.

RASPBERRY LIQUEUR GLAZE
½ cup raspberry liqueur
2 tablespoons redcurrant jelly
2 rounded tablespoons raspberry jelly crystals

In a small saucepan heat raspberry liqueur with red currant jelly. Add jelly crystals and stir until completely dissolved. Allow to cool.

Elaine and Bob Hardy, Thornlea Wines, Sorell Fruit Farm, Sorell

Granita is a relative of sorbet but has an icier and coarser texture and contains less sugar. Serve this fruit liqueur granita over chilled, sweet summer fruits. It can also be used in cocktails as an alternative to crushed ice.

FRUIT LIQUEUR GRANITA
Serves 4

FRUIT LIQUEUR

Pour 1½ cups of your chosen fruit liqueur in a shallow metal container. Place it in the freezer and stir with a fork every 30 minutes. Continue to do this, crushing any large frozen chunks until it is firm but not solid. It usually takes around 3 hours for the desired consistency to be reached. Once the granita is ready it should be served within an hour or so before it freezes into a solid block. To serve, scrape the ice with a fork so that is 'flaky' and place it in a chilled serving container. Serve immediately.

FRUIT LIQUEUR ICE-BLOCKS

Freeze your choice of fruit liqueur in ice-block trays. If you have some of the fun shaped ones, all the better. The frozen blocks make a great addition to chilled summer drinks such as cold fruit teas, milk shakes, and are ideal in punches.

Fruit liqueur can be frozen to make an icy topping for summer fruits and drinks. Serve in small quantities. It can also be combined with pureed, sweetened fruits. For example a strawberry granita would require 2 cups strawberries pureed with ¼ cup castor sugar then combined with 1 cup strawberry liqueur.

Elaine and Bob Hardy, Thornlea Wines, Sorell Fruit Farm, Sorell

FINE APPLE TART
Serves 6

2 cups plain flour
60g (3 tablespoons) sugar
125g (½ cup) butter
water
1kg cooking apples, peeled, cored quartered and cut in fine slices

Mix flour and sugar in a bowl, add soft butter, then water, little by little as necessary to make a pliable dough. Wrap in plastic wrap and chill in the fridge. Roll out dough and use a small bread and butter plate to mark circles in the dough. Place discs on small pizza trays and let them rest in the fridge. When ready to bake, arrange apple slices evenly on the base and cook in a preheated 200°C oven for 20 minutes. Serve hot with a scoop of ice-cream in the middle.

Remi and Ginette Bancal, Peppers Calstock, Deloraine

LEMONGRASS & PALM SUGAR PANNA COTTA with ORANGE & CHILLI CARAMEL, CANDIED CHILLIES & ORANGE ZEST

Serves 7–8

400ml pouring cream
200ml milk
50g castor sugar
75g gula melaka palm sugar
(Available from Asian stores)
1 large stem lemongrass, cut and bruised
1 leaf thick gelatin, or 2 thin leaves

Warm cream and milk and dissolve both the castor and palm sugar well. Add lemongrass and simmer for 10 minutes. Boil briefly, then take off the heat, leaving the lid on to infuse the flavours. Soak gelatin and dissolve it into the mixture last of all. After 30 minutes, strain and pour this mixture into 7 or 8 dariole moulds.

To serve, unmould each panna cotta using a sharp, thin-bladed knife to release. Place onto the centre of the plates. Drizzle orange chilli caramel around each panna cotta and place a piece each of candied chilli and orange zest (recipes follow) on top of each panna cotta.

ORANGE AND CHILLI CARAMEL

1 orange, unpeeled, halved
1 cup castor sugar
220ml water
1 teaspoon glucose
1 chilli, finely chopped and blanched

Dissolve sugar and glucose in the water over low heat. Add the orange and continue to cook until the mixture starts to take on a golden colour, keeping the sides clean by swirling the pan, but do not whisk it! When the caramel has reached the desired colour, remove the orange and cool the pan by setting it in a bowl of tepid water. While the caramel is cooling, add the chilli.

CANDIED CHILLIES & ORANGE ZEST

6 long red mild chillies, halved lengthwise, seeded and sliced in long strips leaving the top intact
zest of 1 orange sliced thinly,
1 cup castor sugar
1 cup water

Blanch chilli twice in boiling water for approximately 30 seconds each time. Blanch the orange zest three times for approximately 30 seconds each time. Make a sugar syrup by boiling the sugar and water together, then cook the chilli and orange zest in that syrup until thoroughly cooked. Take each piece out of the syrup and place on a piece of baking paper, re-shaping a little. Sprinkle with a little castor sugar at serving time.

Don Cameron, Stillwater River Cafe, Launceston

Chef Fiona Hoskin (left) uses honey from Mole Creek for the tuiles, and local berries to go with the panna cotta. 'I had a glut of berries one summer and wanted something creamy but light to accompany them,' she says, when explaining how the dish came about.

VANILLA BEAN PANNA COTTA with BERRIES IN ROSEWATER SYRUP WITH HONEY TUILES

Makes 20 small dariole moulds

3 level teaspoons gelatin powder
4 cups cream
8 gelatin leaves
2 vanilla beans, cut in half lengthwise
400g sugar
5 cups milk

Sprinkle gelatin powder over the cream and stir. Leave to soak for 10 minutes while the gelatin leaves soak in cold water. Scrape out all the vanilla bean seeds, add the seeds and pods to the cream with the sugar and bring to the boil. Squeeze out all water from the gelatin leaves and add to the pan, then remove from the heat. When cool add the milk, strain to remove pods and any skin that might have formed, then pour into lightly oiled dariole moulds and refrigerate to set. To serve, invert each mould onto a plate and serve with berries in rosewater syrup and honey tuiles (recipes follow).

ROSEWATER SYRUP

2 tablespoons cardamom pods
4 cups water
4 cups sugar
2 vanilla beans, halved lengthwise and seeds scraped out
2 cups raspberry juice
3 drops rosewater
150ml lemon juice

Roast cardamom pods in a dry pan over gentle heat until they begin to burst. Cool, then grind in a mortar and pestle. Add to the water, with sugar and vanilla beans. Simmer until reduced and syrupy then add raspberry juice, rosewater and lemon juice to taste. Store with the pods still in the syrup, but sieve before using.

HONEY TUILES

110g castor sugar
1 teaspoon vanilla essence
75g (just over ½ cup)
sifted plain flour
2 eggs
30g very soft butter
2 teaspoons honey

These very versatile wafer thin biscuits make a great dessert garnish. You can set them flat, or wind them around a knife steel to set in a corkscrew shape. They are crisp and delicious, although very fragile to handle.

Place all ingredients into the bowl of a mixer, and beat until just smooth. Spread thinly into long thin shapes on silicone baking sheets or baking paper, and bake in a preheated slow oven until golden brown. Carefully remove with a palette knife and bend into the required shape while still hot. If tuiles go hard before you have shaped them, you can return them briefly to the oven and they will soften again.

Fiona Hoskin, Fee and Me Restaurant, Launceston

Using fresh Tasmanian dairy products and Anvers dark orange chocolate segments, this recipe has been adapted from a traditional chocolate mousse recipe. Chocolatier Igor Van Gerwen says he features this dessert in the House of Anvers cafe and also at demonstrations in major department stores.

MILK CHOCOLATE & TANGERINE MOUSSE

Serves 6

2 gelatin leaves
300ml cream
200g milk chocolate
3 eggs, separated
1 teaspoon castor sugar
tangerine essential oil
300ml cream
1 tablespoon sugar
natural vanilla essence, as desired
grated citrus zest
dark orange chocolate segments for decoration

Soak gelatin in cold water for 5 minutes, drain and add a dash of boiling water until all gelatin is melted.

Make ganache by gently heating 100ml of cream with the milk chocolate. Stir until glossy, then mix in egg yolks and gelatin. Flavour to taste with tangerine oil.

Semi-whip the remaining 200ml of cream. In a separate bowl (making sure whisk and bowl are grease-free to achieve maximum volume) beat egg whites with sugar until soft peaks form. Fold ganache into the softly whipped cream. Fold in egg whites. Scoop into glasses and chill until set. Semi-whip the additional cream required for the garnish with sugar and vanilla essence.

To serve, top the set mousse with whipped cream, citrus zest and dark orange chocolate segments as decoration.

Igor Van Gerwen, Anvers Confectionery Pty Ltd, Latrobe

What began as a super-simple idea has given this tomato farm a new direction. And whoever thought of using tomatoes as a dessert? 'Enjoy the 'simple mystery delight' when tried,' says Marilyn Lanyon.

'SIMPLY' DELICATE ICE-CREAM   Makes 2 litres

2 litres raspberry or strawberry ice-cream
4 tablespoons of Simply Green Tomatoes (drained)
(The reserved oil can be used for pan frying or in salad dressing)

Finely chop the Simply Green Tomatoes and mix through softened ice-cream. Place back into freezer and re-chill. Serve with your favourite dessert or in an ice-cream cone.

Marilyn Lanyon, Simply Tomatoes, Boort

Remember to use only blue L.angustifolia lavender flowers for cooking.

LAVENDER CHEESECAKE

1 mug crushed biscuit crumbs (Marie biscuits)
150g butter, melted
125g Philadelphia cream cheese, warmed
½ cup sugar
1 mug cream
1 mug milk
3½ teaspoons gelatin
fresh blue L.angustifolia lavender or borage flowers

Mix biscuit crumbs and butter together to make a firm mixture. Line a well-greased 22cm springform pan or flan dish with biscuit mix. Mix cream cheese and sugar, add cream and milk, and beat together. Dissolve gelatin in a little hot water and add to this mixture, allow it to stand until it begins to set. Pour cooled mixture over the biscuit base and top with a sprinkle of lavender flowers. Cover and chill in fridge overnight.

Serve topped with piped whipped cream. Decorate with lavender or borage flowers. Refrigerate leftover cheesecake.

Rosemary Holmes, Yuulong Lavender Estate, Mount Egerton

Yarra Valley and the Dandenong Ranges: one of the food bowl regions of Australia, famous for its boutique vineyards and produce (above, from Yering Station).

This makes a scrumptious addition to fresh fruit.

RASPBERRY YOGHURT DESSERT Serves 4

1 cup of thick plain yoghurt
4 tablespoons castor sugar
grated rind of ½ lemon
1 cup cream
1 cup raspberries
100g grated 'Energy' (dark eating)
chocolate

Mix yoghurt, sugar and lemon rind, then add cream. Fork the raspberries through the mixture and fold in chocolate.

Tracey Molloy, Kinglake Raspberries, Pheasant Creek

'We serve this at least once a week, usually with home-made ice-cream. We always have half a dozen in the freezer. Quantities are large,' says Annabelle Abbotts, 'as we are usually catering for a large group, but this recipe can easily be reduced to a manageable quantity to feed six or so!'

CHOCOLATE, DATE & ALMOND TORTE   Serves 12

250g slivered or flaked almonds
250g dark chocolate, broken into pieces
6 egg whites
125g castor sugar
250g dates or figs, chopped finely

Grease a foil-lined 23cm cake tin. Place almonds and chocolate in a food processor and chop into chunky pieces. Beat egg whites until stiff peaks form, and then add castor sugar, beating in well. Combine with the dates, chocolate and almonds, pour into the tin and bake in a preheated 180°C oven for approximately 45 minutes. When done, open the oven door slightly and allow to cool in the pan. Turn onto a platter when cooled and chill in the fridge.

Annabelle Abbotts, Mt Hart Wilderness Lodge, Kimberley

Biscuits

According to Annette Greenhalgh, this is 'a great biscuit recipe and children in particular love them. This recipe was given to me many, many years ago by an Italian lady, called Franca, who lives next door to my parents at Hanwood, near Griffith in the Riverina. Franca is happy to share it.'

LEMON BISCOTTI   Makes approximately 50 biscuits

5 eggs
1½ cups white sugar
¾ cup vegetable oil
4 cups self raising flour
few drops of lemon essence (or
substitute rosewater or orange
flower essence)
1½ cups icing sugar for coating

Line two biscuit trays with baking paper. Separate egg whites and yolks. Beat egg whites until soft peaks form. Add egg yolks, sugar, oil, flour and lemon essence, folding in with a spatula until mixture resembles a very soft dough. Lightly roll tablespoons of mixture into balls and coat in icing sugar. Place on trays. Bake 15–20 minutes in preheated 180°C oven. Cool on rack. Biscuits will keep well for about 2 weeks if stored in an airtight container.

*Annette Greenhalgh, Duck Under the Table, Cheesemaking &
Cookery School, Wingham*

LEMON & LAVENDER SHORTBREAD TALINGA GROVE

Makes about 24

150g castor sugar
300g plain flour
50g cornflour
125g butter, softened
100ml Talinga Grove lemon-infused
olive oil
2 teaspoons dried lavender flowers,
crushed,
(use only blue L.angustifolia lavender)
2 teaspoons vanilla extract
55g semolina
icing sugar

Sift sugar, flour and cornflour together. Beat butter in mixer on low speed until creamy. Continue mixing on low speed and slowly add the lemon-infused olive oil until combined. Add sugar, sifted flours, lavender, vanilla extract and semolina, then mix with a wooden spoon. Allow to come together like a dough, then wrap in cling-film and refrigerate for 2 hours.

Remove from fridge and let rest for 10 minutes. Roll out thinly to 1cm thickness and cut with a biscuit cutter. Bake in a preheated 150°C oven for about 30 minutes or until slightly golden. Cool on wire tray and serve dusted with icing sugar.

Helen Morgan, Talinga Grove, Strathalbyn

According to Ingrid Glastonbury, 'this recipe would have been brought out from Germany (or Prussia as it was at the time) by the Riedel family, and handed down to Melva Rothe who gave the recipe to my mother, Irma Dallwitz.' For easier handling, roll out the biscuit dough between sheets of greaseproof paper.

ZIMMT STERNE ('CINNAMON STARS') Makes approx 30

3 egg whites
300g icing sugar
300g fine almond meal
2 level teaspoons ground cinnamon
½ teaspoon ground cardamom
juice of ½ lemon

Beat egg whites stiffly and mix in the icing sugar gradually until well combined. Divide into two separate quantities, one with ⅓ the mixture, one with ⅔ the mixture (do this by weighing the meringue mixture). Now mix almond meal and spices into the ⅔ meringue mixture. Mix well, then add lemon juice and mix again. Set aside for 30 minutes.

Knead well (this will be easier if you use some almond meal to keep the mixture from sticking to your hands. Roll out to about 1cm thickness and cut into stars. Brush the tops with the ⅓ meringue mixture. Bake in a slow (145°C, fan-forced) oven for 10 minutes.

Ingrid Glastonbury, Krondorf Road Cafe,
Kabminye Wines, Krondorf

Cakes and breads

This recipe features Reinette de Angleterre, a heritage apple variety grown at Borrodell on the Mount, which produces 170 varieties of heritage apples.

SISTERS ROCK APPLE CAKE

100g unsalted butter
100ml milk
1 teaspoon vanilla essence
100g (¾ cup) plain flour
2 teaspoons baking powder
pinch salt
1 egg
100g sugar
1kg Reinette de Angleterre apples, peeled, cored quartered and cut into thin slices

Melt butter with milk in a saucepan. Do not allow to boil. Add vanilla essence. Sift flour and baking powder into a bowl. Adding a pinch of salt and using an electric mixer, beat the egg and sugar until light and foamy then combine with the flour, and milk and butter mixture. Finally add the apples and stir well. Butter a 23cm cake tin and line with baking paper. Pour mixture in pan and spread evenly. Bake in a preheated oven at 175°C for approximately 1 hour.

Marina Fedele and Patricia Fiorini, Sisters Rock Cafe,
Borrodell on the Mount, Orange

'This is adapted from an old Italian chocolate bread recipe,' says Paul Wilderbeek (below). 'As with all my breads this recipe was as the result of 'trying to do something different' and trial and error which we like to call product development.'

BELGIAN CHOCOLATE BREAD
Makes 3 loaves

500g (4 cups) strong baker's flour
2 teaspoons salt
2 teaspoons dry yeast
1¼ tablespoons olive oil
300ml warm water
500g dark Belgian couverture chocolate (as callets or small chocolate buttons)
chocolate icing
(mix icing sugar and water and coca)
white icing
(mix icing sugar and water)

Place flour, salt, yeast, oil and water into a mixer and, using a dough hook, slowly work the ingredients into a dough. It should take about 10 minutes on a slow speed. Add the chocolate to this basic dough and mix until it is very well combined, about another 4-5mins. Place dough into a lightly greased bowl and cover with plastic wrap or a damp tea towel and prove in a warm place until it doubles in size, normally about an hour. This time will depend on air temperature and the temperature of the dough.

Remove from the bowl and knock out the air that has formed in the dough. Divide the dough into three and shape into ball shapes. This takes a little practice to get the surface nice and smooth. Place on a greased baking tray or a tray covered with baking paper.

When the loaves have doubled in size again, place them into a preheated 185°C oven for about 20 minutes, depending on your oven. Cool on a wire rack. When cold decorate with the two water icings. Serve with coffee or just on its own.

PAUL'S BREAD-MAKING TIPS
- Ensure water temperature is nice and warm to activate the yeast cells.
- Make sure the dough doubles before knocking back and shaping.
- Ensure oven is hot before placing bread in.
- Do not try to put icing on hot bread.

Paul Wilderbeek, Proven Artisan Breads and Pastries, Orange

CITRUS TWIST CAKE

Serves 10

250g butter
1¼ cups caster sugar
1 tablespoon finely shredded lemon zest
2 free-range eggs, separated
2 tablespoons cooled, strained Citrus Twist tea
(Available from Simon Johnson and other fine food providores.)
2 teaspoons Boyajian lemon oil or 1 tablespoon finely shredded lemon zest
(Available from Simon Johnson and other fine food providores.)
1½ cups Greek-style yoghurt
2½ cups self raising flour

Preheat oven to 180°C and grease a 26cm round cake tin. In a large bowl cream together butter, sugar and lemon zest until light and fluffy. Add egg yolks slowly, one at a time, beating between each addition.

Combine the tea, lemon oil (or extra zest if not available) and yoghurt in a separate bowl and mix well, then combine the yoghurt mixture and egg batter and fold in the flour. In a separate bowl beat eggwhites until stiff then fold gently into batter.

Pour the mixture into the prepared tin and bake in the pre-heated oven for 1 hour or until cake is risen and set. Transfer to a rack to cool, leaving the cake in the tin. Pour the syrup (recipe follows) over the cake while it is still warm and leave to cool. Remove cake from tin and transfer to a serving platter.

SYRUP

finely grated zest and juice of 2 lemons
1 cup sugar
1 cup strained Citrus Twist tea

Place the zest, lemon juice, sugar and Citrus Twist tea into a saucepan. Bring to the boil over low heat, then remove from the heat and allow the syrup to cool.

Suzy Martin, The Herb Barn Pty Ltd, Tatong

'This cake freezes well,' says Rosemary. 'Warmed fruitcake served with ice-cream or cream makes a good dessert. We make this cake constantly.'

LAVENDER FRUITCAKE

500g mixed fruit
125g butter
1 cup brown sugar
1 teaspoon mixed spice
1 cup water
1 teaspoon bicarbonate of soda
1 tablespoon blue L.angustifolia lavender flowers
2 eggs
½ cup brandy or sherry
1 cup self raising flour
1 cup plain flour

Grease and line a 20cm cake tin. Place fruit, butter, sugar, spice and water in a saucepan and heat gently until butter is melted. Bring to the boil and simmer 5 minutes. When mixture has cooled add bicarbonate of soda and lavender flowers, then eggs and brandy or sherry, mixing in well. Sift flours and add to the mixture, stirring in well. Pour into the prepared tin and bake in a preheated moderate 190°C oven for 1½–2 hours. Test with a skewer after cake has been cooking for an hour. Leave in tin until cold.

Rosemary Holmes, Yuulong Lavender Estate, Mount Egerton

'The Willamette variety of raspberry has been in Australia since the 1940s,' says Tracey Molloy. 'It has a deep claret colour when fully ripe and displays an exquisite raspberry taste.'

RASPBERRY & BANANA MUFFINS   Makes 6 large or 12 small muffins

1½ cups self raising flour
¼ teaspoon salt
1 cup raw sugar
2 tablespoons melted butter
¾ cup milk
1 egg, beaten
1 cup fresh or frozen raspberries, preferably Williamette
2 over-ripe bananas, mashed
brown sugar to sprinkle

Mix flour, salt and sugar together. Melt butter, mix with milk, add egg and mix well. Using a knife, stir milk mixture into flour until just mixed, but still lumpy. Mix raspberries and banana into mixture with knife—be careful not to over-mix. Spoon into prepared muffin pans, sprinkle with brown sugar, and bake in a preheated 200°C oven until golden brown, for 15-20 minutes.

Tracey Molloy, Kinglake Raspberries, Pheasant Creek

'My mother was a terrible cook,' says Ann Creber, 'but happily, Nanna, who lived with us, was passionate about growing her own food and then using it to the best possible advantage. My special favourite was her Spanish Walnut Cake. She would never divulge her recipe but long after Marzie had died, my aunt shared it with me. It has become a family favourite, cooked for special occasions, and is just as good as my childhood recollections of it. The cake itself is easy to make but the caramel frosting takes a bit of time and effort, even with an electric beater.'

SPANISH WALNUT CAKE

1 cup self raising flour
1 tablespoon ground cinnamon (yes, a tablespoon!)
125g butter, softened
¾ cup dark brown sugar
2 eggs, separated
½ cup milk
¾ cup chopped walnuts

Sift together flour and cinnamon. Beat together butter and sugar until thoroughly creamed, add egg yolks and beat mixture again. Gradually stir milk into the creamed mixture. Fold in flour and cinnamon, then add walnuts. Beat egg whites until stiff, then gently but thoroughly fold into other ingredients. Carefully spoon into a buttered and floured loaf tin and cook in preheated 180°C oven for 35-45 minutes. Remove from tin and cool on a wire rack. Cover with Caramel Frosting when quite cold.

CARAMEL FROSTING

2 cups dark brown sugar
½ cup milk
125g butter
1 teaspoon vanilla essence
walnut halves or chopped walnuts

Combine sugar, milk and butter in a saucepan. Cook over moderate heat until mixture forms a ball when dropped into cold water. Brush down the inside of the saucepan with a little cold water from time to time. Cool a little, then add the vanilla essence. Beat (and beat and beat!) until thick and of a spreading consistency. Frost the entire cake and garnish with walnut halves or chopped walnuts. For easy slicing, dip a sharp knife into hot water before cutting the cake.

Ann Creber, Whispers From Provence, Kalorama

For an added touch for presentation, saute some peeled and cored apple quarters in some butter and place them onto the bottom of the cake tin in a decorative pattern before pouring in the cake batter. Invert to serve.

FOREST GROVE APPLE CAKE

3 cups sliced apples
5 tablespoons sugar
5 teaspoons cinnamon
4 eggs
2 cups sugar
1 cup fruity olive oil
½ cup orange juice
1 teaspoon vanilla essence
3 cups self raising flour, sifted

Mix sliced apples, 5 tablespoons sugar and cinnamon in a bowl and leave for at least 30 minutes. Beat together eggs and sugar until creamy. Add olive oil, orange juice and vanilla, then fold in sifted flour.

Pour half the mixture into a large springform cake tin or large baking dish which has been greased and lined with baking paper. Spoon the sliced apples and cinnamon over, then top with remaining cake batter. Bake in a preheated moderate oven for about an hour or until a skewer comes out clean when inserted in the centre. Remove from pan and cool on a rack.

Jill James, Forest Grove Olive Oil Farm, Margaret River

SOUTH AUSTRALIA Adelaide Hills

'This bread is excellent served with paté,' says Deborah Cantrill. 'I like to experiment, so I added some chestnuts to my regular bread recipe. I like it whenever we have goose liver paté, which is several times a year, but I have also made it for morning tea on sunny autumn days.'

CHESTNUT BREAD

Makes 24 medium sized rolls or 30 small rolls

500g (4 cups) flour
1 tablespoon dried yeast
4 tablespoons chestnut flour
(Available from speciality stores)
1 teaspoon salt
approx. 2 cups warm water
1 teaspoon malt extract
½ tablespoon olive oil
1 cup fresh chestnuts cooked, peeled and chopped into small pieces (or use dried chestnuts, soaked, then cooked)
milk or beaten egg

Mix together flour, yeast, chestnut flour and salt. Add water and malt extract, oil and chestnuts. Knead well and allow to rise for one hour. Shape into small rolls, then cover and allow to rise another 20 minutes. Glaze with milk or beaten egg and bake in a preheated 240°C oven for 10-12 minutes. Cool on a rack.

Deborah Cantrill, Nirvana Organic Produce, Heathfield

Jams, relishes and spreads

Pinnacle Berries

Blue Noise Jam
245gm

Adrienne Newman says 'The olive trees at Sandalyn Estate are among the first planted in the Hunter Valley. The species, Olea europaea, *originated in Africa 6,000 years ago and are the oldest trees under cultivation in the world. Apart from pickling our olives, we make tapenade to eat with wood fired bread and a glass of Sandalyn's Traditional Methode Champenoise.'*

OLIVE TAPENADE
Makes about 1 cup

800g olives black olives, pitted
4 cloves garlic (or more to taste)
4 anchovy fillets
4 tablespoons capers, rinsed and squeezed dry
4 teaspoons chopped fresh thyme
2 tablespoons lemon juice
½ cup extra virgin olive oil (an early harvest like Olio Mio)
salt and pepper

Put all ingredients into a blender and process. Adjust seasoning. Spoon into a container and top with more olive oil. You may experiment by adding some Dijon mustard and some chopped fresh rosemary as liked. Enjoy spread on fresh bread or as an addition to many dishes.

Adrienne Newman, The Olive and the Grape, Sandalyn Estate, Lovedale.

'Do not slice the ricotta too thickly,' is the advice for this useful condiment that will go with many dishes, or simply as an addition to a sandwich or bruschetta.

KENILWORTH MARINATED FETA
Makes about 1 cup

200g Kenilworth Feta, cut into bite-size cubes
4 garlic cloves, crushed
2 tablespoons finely cut fresh basil
olive oil

Mix the cubed feta together with the garlic and basil. Sprinkle olive oil over the mixture. Cover and place in the refrigerator for an hour before serving. Use on salads or other dishes.

Henry Gosling, Kenilworth Country Foods Pty Ltd, Kenilworth

Lynette Klavins says that this relish is sweet with a slight chilli after-burn and works wonderfully with cold lamb or ham. Put a pot on a cheese platter to spread on crisp lavosh slices.

FIG, RAISIN & CHILLI RELISH
Makes ten 200g jars

1 kg ripe figs
350g raisins
300g onions, chopped
500g brown sugar
2 cups malt vinegar
1 level teaspoon ground pimento
1 level teaspoon ground cinnamon
1 heaped teaspoon salt
1 heaped teaspoon chilli flakes
1 heaped teaspoon crushed garlic
1 heaped teaspoon ginger
½ teaspoon blade mace
or ground mace

Combine all ingredients in a saucepan, bring to the boil and cook gently for 1½ hours. Use a stick blender to combine ingredients into a thick paste (or use a food processor). Bottle and seal while hot. Use within 18 months of bottling. Refrigerate after opening.

Lynette Klavins, Penna Lane Wines, Clare

'Make this in summer or autumn when rhubarb is plentiful' says Lynette Klavins. 'The rich creamy texture of the rhubarb matches well with the semillon. It's fantastic with wedges of soft cheese.'

RHUBARB & SEMILLON RELISH
Makes eight 200g jars

1 bunch (approx 1kg) fresh rhubarb, washed and trimmed
1 large onion, finely chopped
2 tablespoons grated ginger
2 tablespoons crushed garlic
2 cups Penna Lane Semillon
2 cups good malt vinegar
grated rind and juice of 1 lemon
grated rind and juice of 1 orange
1 tablespoon salt
800g brown sugar
500g raisins

Cut the rhubarb into 2cm pieces. Combine rhubarb, onion, ginger, garlic, wine, vinegar, and citrus rind and juice with the salt in a large saucepan. Bring to the boil, then add sugar and raisins. Stir to dissolve the sugar. Cook very slowly until the mixture is thick, stirring often to ensure it doesn't burn. Bottle and seal when hot.

This can be used straight away, but benefits by a couple of weeks maturing to allow the flavours to combine most effectively. Use within 18 months of bottling. Refrigerate after opening.

Lynette Klavins , Penna Lane Wines, Clare

'The peppery and spicy berry fruit of the shiraz works well with the tartness of the Morello cherries from our tree and the richness of the plums and spices,' says Lynette Klavins. 'Serve with cold meats, especially ham off the bone or continental sausages.'

SPICY PLUM, CHERRY & SHIRAZ RELISH

Makes about nine 200g jars

1kg red plums (blood plums are best), stoned and halved

500g sour cherries, stoned

375ml Penna Lane Shiraz

350g brown onions, chopped

2 tablespoons peeled and grated fresh ginger

½ cup white wine vinegar

1 tablespoon prepared horseradish

1 tablespoon seeded mustard

3 red chillies, finely chopped

2 teaspoons salt

1 teaspoon ground cardamom

½ teaspoon ground allspice

pinch ground cloves

400g brown sugar

Place the plums and cherries in a large saucepan with the rest of the ingredients except for the sugar. Bring to the boil, then add the sugar and stir until it is dissolved. Cook over medium heat until reduced to a thick mixture—about an hour. Bottle and seal when hot. Leave for at least a month for the flavours to combine and mature, but use within 18 months of bottling. Refrigerate after opening.

Lynette Klavins, Penna Lane Wines, Clare

Chef Martin Gillespie says, 'I was messing around with a salad dressing using local olives, lemons, fresh herbs and olive oil from the Frankland River region. For more flavour, adding garlic, anchovies and capers just finished it off. A great dip or dressing, whether for a cold salad in summer or a warm salad in winter.'

WARM CHUNKY OLIVE TAPENADE   Makes about 1 cup

2 large garlic cloves, chopped
a good glug of Jingilli olive oil from the Frankland River region (Gillespie suggests a Frantoio or Leccino)
8 anchovy fillets, roughly chopped
¼ cup capers roughly chopped
rind of half a lemon, finely chopped
150g Moore River table olives, pitted and roughly chopped
fresh parsley or marjoram to taste, roughly chopped

Place garlic, olive oil, anchovies, capers and lemon rind in a frying pan and warm gently until garlic is toasted. Add olives and chopped herbs and continue to warm for a further minute.

NOTE: This dip can be chunky or smooth (in the latter case, whiz in a food processor) depending how you require the tapenade, and can also double up as a great salad dressing.

Martin Gillespie, Waddi Bush Resort, Badgingarra

Serve warm with flat bread and a glass of Pinot Noir from Salitage Pemberton.

Drinks

The Colletts claim that 'limes are a magic green health tablet—full of vitamin C and anti-inflammatory flavonoids'. What's more, the cordial they make has party aspirations too!

THE WORLD'S BEST DAIQUIRI

Make drinks to these proportions:
⅓ Lime Grove Pure Lime Juice Cordial-Heaven in a Bottle
⅓ vodka or Bacardi
⅓ crushed ice

Mix together thoroughly in a cocktail shaker.

Serve in cocktail glass with a thin slice of lime perched on the edge of the glass.

Peter and Susie Collett, Lime Grove, Narromine

VICTORIA Legends, Wine and High Country

This refreshing drink is based on a delightful, tangy tea.

CITRUS TWIST ICED TEA   Serves 4

1 cup water
1 cup sugar
4 tablespoons Citrus Twist loose tea
6 cups of water
juice of 1 lemon
fresh lemon verbena or mint
lemon slices

Place water and sugar in a saucepan. Allow mixture to come to the boil, then reduce heat to a simmer until sugar is completely dissolved. Cool syrup and refrigerate until required. Place cold water and loose tea in a large jug and stir. Chill for 12 hours.

To strain tea, pour through paper filter or a plunger not previously used for coffee. Add the lemon juice into the iced tea. Add sugar syrup according to taste. Pour 2 cups of the iced tea into ice cube trays and freeze, then chill the remainder. When ready to serve, place ice cubes into a jug, pour chilled tea over, then add fresh lemon verbena or mint and lemon slices.

Suzy Martin, The Herb Barn Pty Ltd, Tatong

Australian Regional Producers and Chefs

Annabelle Abbotts
Mt Hart Wilderness Lodge
Gibb River Road,
Kimberley, WA, 6728
Phone: 08 9191 4545
www.mthart.com.au

Jill Allanson
Lyndoch Lavender Farm and Cafe
Corner Hoffnungsthal and
Tweedies Gully Roads,
PO Box 68, Lyndoch, SA, 5351
Phone: 08 8524 4538
www.lyndochlavenderfarm.com.au

Anne Ashbolt
Ashbolt Farm
PO Box 21, Plenty, Tas, 7140
Phone: 03 6261 2203

Cort Assenheim, Executive Chef
Seabelle Restaurant
Kingfisher Bay Resort, Fraser
Island, Qld, 4655
PMB 1 Urangan, Qld, 4655
Phone: 07 4120 3333
www.kingfisherbay.com

Remi and Ginette Bancal
Peppers Calstock
Highland Lakes Road, Deloraine,
Tasmania, 7304
Phone: 03 6362 2642
www.peppers.com.au/calstock

Barbara Barlin
Barbushco Pty Ltd
50 Gills Rd, Lorne, NSW, 2439
Phone: 02 6556 9656
www.barbushco.com.au

Paul Benhaim
Alive Foods
14 Boongala Avenue,
Montville, Qld, 4560
Phone: 0407 767 709
www.alivefoods.com
www.notthecookingshow.com

Helen Brierty and Annette Fear
Spirit House Restaurant and
Cooking School.
20 Ninderry Road,
Yandina, Qld, 4561
PO Box 268, Yandina, Qld, 4561
Phone: 07 5446 8977
www.spirithouse.com.au

Sally Brinsmead
Tropical Fruit World
Duranbah Rd,
Duranbah, NSW, 2487
Phone: 02 6677 7222
www.tropicalfruitworld.com.au

Gordon Brown
Evelyn County Estate's
Black Paddock Restaurant
55 Eltham-Yarra Glen Road,
Kangaroo Ground, Victoria, 3097
Phone: 03 9437 2155
www.evelyncountyestate.com.au

Don Cameron, Chef
Stillwater River Cafe
PO Box 377
bottom of Paterson Street,
Launceston,
Tasmania, 7250
Phone: 03 6331 4153
www.stillwater.net.au

Todd Cameron, Head Chef
Gaia Retreat and Spa
PO Box 304, Bangalow, NSW, 2479
Phone: 02 6687 1216
www.gaiaretreat.com.au

Deborah Cantrill
Nirvana Organic Produce
184 Longwood Rd,
Heathfield, SA, 5153
Phone: 08 8339 2519

Donna Carrier
Bent on Food Regional Produce
Store
22 Bent St, Wingham, NSW, 2429
Phone: 02 6557 0727

Marion Chambers
Penguin Stop Cafe
Middle Terrace, Penneshaw,
Kangaroo Island, SA, 5222
Phone: 08 8553 1211

Peter and Susie Collett, Lime Grove
4606 Mitchell Hwy,
Narromine, NSW, 2821
Phone: 02 6889 1962
www.limegrove.net.au

Vanessa Cox
Mudgee Gourmet Hazelnuts
8 Court Street, Mudgee, NSW, 2850

Phone: 02 6372 3224
www.mudgeegourmet.com.au
(consumer)
www.gourmethazelnuts.com.au
(trade)

Ann Creber
Whispers From Provence
41-45 Barbers Rd, Kalorama,
Victoria, 3766
Phone: 03 9728 4475

Bechora Deeb, Chef
Deeb's Kitchen
Cnr Cassilis Rd and Buckeroo Lane
PO Box 949
Mudgee, NSW, 2850
Phone: 02 6373 3133
www.homestead.com/deeb-
skitchen/index.html

Marina Fedele and Patricia Fiorini,
Sisters Rock Cafe,
Borrodell on the Mount,
Lake Canobolas Road,
Orange, NSW, 2800
Phone: 02 6365 3425
www.borrodell.com.au

Grosvenor and Ro Francis, John
Grant
High Valley Wine and Cheese
137 Cassilis Rd,
Mudgee, NSW, 2850
Phone: 02 6372 1011
www.highvalley.com.au

Martin Gillespie
Waddi Bush Resort,
Badgingarra, WA, 6521
Phone: 08 9652 9071
www.bushresorts.com.au

Ingrid Glastonbury
Krondorf Road Cafe
Kabminye Wines,
PO Box 629, Krondorf Road,
Krondorf near Tanunda, SA, 5352
Phone: 08 8563 0889
www.kabminye.com

Les and Darilyn Goldsmith
Goldsmith's in the Forest
Harrison's Track,
Lakes Entrance, Vic, 3909
Phone: 03 5155 2518
www.goldsmithsintheforest.com.au

Henry Gosling
General Manager
Kenilworth Country Foods Pty Ltd
PO Box 45
45 Charles Street,
Kenilworth, Qld, 4574
Phone: 07 5446 0144
coollum.com.au/tourist attractions/Kenilworth

Annette Greenhalgh
Duck Under the Table,
Cheesemaking and Cookery School
22 Bent Street,
Wingham, NSW, 2429
Phone: 02 655 70409
www.duckunder.com

Marion Hansford and Stewart Gilchrist
The Pickled Sisters Cafe
Distillery Road,
Wahgunyah, Vic, 3687
Phone: 02 6033 2377

Elaine and Bob Hardy
Thornlea Wines, Sorell Fruit Farm
174 Pawleena Road,
Sorell, Tas, 7172
Phone: 03 6265 2744
www.sorellfruitfarm.com

Justin Harris, Executive Chef
Source Restaurant
Moorilla Estate, 655 Main Road,
Berriedale, Tas, 7011
Phone: 03 6277 9900
www.moorilla.com.au

Nigel Harvey, Executive Chef,
Voyager Estate Winery,
Lot 1, Stevens Rd,
Margaret River, WA, 6285
Phone: 08 9757 6354
www.voyagerestate.com.au

Rosemary Holmes
Yuulong Lavender Estate
58 Sharrocks Rd,
Mount Egerton, Vic, 3352
Phone: 03 5368 9453
www.ballarat.com/yuulon

Richard Hooper, Executive Chef
Pettavel Winery and Restaurant
65 Pettavel Road,
Waurn Ponds, Vic, 3216
Phone: 03 5266 1120
www.pettavel.com

Fiona Hoskin, Chef
Fee and Me Restaurant
190 Charles Street,
Launceston, Tas, 7250
Phone: 03 6331 3195
www.feeandme.com.au

Jill James,
Forest Grove Olive Oil Farm,
Margaret River
RMB 317, Harrison Road,
Forest Grove, WA, 6286
Phone: 08 9757 6428
www.forestgroveolives.com.au

John Kelly and Katrina McKay
Lenah Game and Gourmet
PO Box 294, Mowbray, Tas, 7248
Phone: 03 6326 7696

Mark and Annette Kern
Bush Rock Cafe
198 Evans Lookout Rd,
Blackheath, NSW, 2785
Phone: 02 4787 7111

Gabrielle Kervella
Kervella Cheese
9 Clenton Road,
Gidgegannup, WA, 6083
Phone: 08 9574 7160 or 08 9574 7092

Lynette Klavins
Penna Lane Wines,
Box 428, Clare, SA, 5453
Phone: 08 8843 4364
www.pennalanewines.com.au

Dennis and Peta Klumpp
King Island Produce
1419 North Rd,
King Island, Tas, 7256
PO Box 280, Currie, 7256
Phone: 03 6463 1147
www.kip.com.au

John Knoll,
Mt Rael Retreat
140 Healesville-Yarra Glen Rd,
Healesville, Vic, 3777
Phone: 03 5962 1977
www.zarliving.com.au

Marilyn Lanyon
Simply Tomatoes
PO Box 176, Boort, Vic, 3537
Phone: 03 5455 4237
www.simplytomatoes.com.au

Brad Lobb, Executive Chef
Campaspe Country House
Goldies Lane, Woodend, Vic, 3422
Phone: 03 5427 2273
www.campaspehouse.com.au

Kas Martin
Chef-Manager, Cafe Y
Yaldara Estates,
Hermann Thumm Dr,
Lyndoch, SA, 5351
Phone: 08 8524 0250
www.yaldara.com.au

Suzy Martin
The Herb Barn Pty Ltd
280 Martins Road,
Tatong, Vic, 3673
Phone: 03 5767 2115

Bernard McCarthy, Chef Proprietor,
Salix Restaurant
Willow Creek Winery, 166
Balnarring Rd,
Merricks North, Vic, 3926
Phone: 03 5989 7640
www.willow-creek.com.au

Tracey Molloy
Kinglake Raspberries
Toohey's Road
Pheasant Creek, Vic, 3757
Phone: 03 5786 5360
www.kinglake-raspberries.com.au

Helen Morgan
Talinga Grove
Talinga Road,
Strathalbyn, SA, 5255
Phone: 08 8536 3911
www.talinga.com.au

Roberta Muir, Director
Sydney Seafood School
Locked Bag 247,
Pyrmont, NSW, 2009
Phone: 02 9004 1111
www.sydneyfishmarket.com.au

Stephen Neale
Three Snails Restaurant
PO Box 734
Riverview Business Park
Darling Street, Dubbo, NSW, 2830
Phone: 02 6884 9994
www.threesnails.com.au

Adrienne Newman
The Olive and the Grape
Sandalyn Estate,
168 Wilderness Rd,
Lovedale, NSW, 2320
Phone: 02 9340 7245
www.theoliveandthegrape.com
www.pennalanewines.com.au

Ros O'Bryan, Olson Game Birds
2167 Chillingollah Rd,
Swan Hill, Vic, 3585
Phone: 03 5030 2648
www.gamebirds.com.au

Robert Salmon, Head Chef
The Silos Restaurant
B640 Princess Hwy,
Jaspers Brush, NSW, 2535
Phone: 02 4448 6160
www.silos.com.au

Jess Scarce
La Trattoria, Lavandula
350 Hepburn-Newstead Road,
Shepherd's Flat, Vic, 3461
Phone: 03 5476 4393
www.lavandula.com.au

Kane Shaw, Chef
Flooded Gums Restaurant
PO Box 9
Bonville International Golf Resort,
Bonville, NSW, 2441
Phone: 02 6653 4002
www.bonvillegolf.com.au

Steven Snow, Chef-owner
Fins Seafood Restaurant
Waterfront Beach Hotel
Bay St, Byron Bay, NSW, 2481
Phone: 02 6685 5029
www.fins.com.au

Ulli Spranz
B.-d. Farm Paris Creek Pty. Ltd,
PO Box 22, Meadows, SA, 5201
Phone: 08 8388 3339
www.bdfarmpariscreek.com.au

Craig Squire
Managing Director
Red Ochre Grill
43 Shields St, Cairns, Qld, 4870
Phone: 07 4051 0100

Bradley Teale
Esca Bimbadgen
790 McDonalds Road,
Pokolbin, NSW, 2321
Phone: 02 4998 4666
www.bimbadgen.com.au

Warren Thompson, Executive Chef
Big Fish
Shoal Bay Resort and Spa,
Beachfront, Shoal Bay, NSW, 2315
Phone: 02 4984 8154
www.shoalbayresort.com

Jerome Tremoulet, Executive Chef,
Penfolds Magill Estate Restaurant
78 Penfold Road, Magill, SA, 5072
Phone: 08 8301 5551
www.penfolds.com.au

Aaron Turner, Chef
Julian's Restaurant at Bellarine
2270 Portarlington Road,
Bellarine, Vic, 3222
Phone: 03 5259 3310
www.bellarineestate.com.au

Igor Van Gerwen
Anvers Confectionery Pty Ltd,
9025 Bass Hwy, Latrobe, Tas, 7307
Phone: 03 6426 2703
www.anvers-chocolate.com.au

Sheldon Wearne
2 Fish Restaurant Cairns
Pier Shopping,
Pier Point Road, Cairns, Qld, 4870
Phone: 07 4041 5350
Shop 7/20 Wharf Street,
Port Douglas, Qld, 4877
Phone: 07 4099 6350
www.2fishrestaurant.com.au

Jane Westcott
Perenti Cafe and Catering
69 Church St,
Gloucester, NSW, 2422
Phone: 02 6558 9219
www.perenti.com.au

Matthew Wild, Wild at Byron
The Byron at Byron
77-99 Broken Head Road,
Byron Bay, NSW, 2481
Phone: 1300 554 362
www.thebyronatbyron.com.au

Paul Wilderbeek
Proven Artisan Breads and Pastries
26B Sale St, Orange, NSW, 2800
Phone: 02 6360 0722

Alla Wolf-Tasker, Chef-owner
Lake House, King St,
Daylesford, Vic, 3460
Phone: 03 5348 3329
www.lakehouse.com.au

Anna Wong and Jerry Mouzakis
Neila Restaurant
5 Kendal Street, Cowra, NSW, 2794
Phone: 02 6341 2188
www.neila.com.au

Kate Woodward, Managing
Director
Hunter Belle Cheese
'Verona'
New England Hwy,
Muswellbrook, NSW, 2333
PO Box 87, Scone, NSW, 2337
Phone: 02 6541 5066
www.hunterbellecheese.com.au

Wolfgang Zichy, Chef
The Moorings Restaurant and Cafe
5/8-10 Electra Parade,
Harrington, NSW, 2427
Phone: 02 6556 1898
www.harringtonwaters.com.au/
moorings

Australian regions

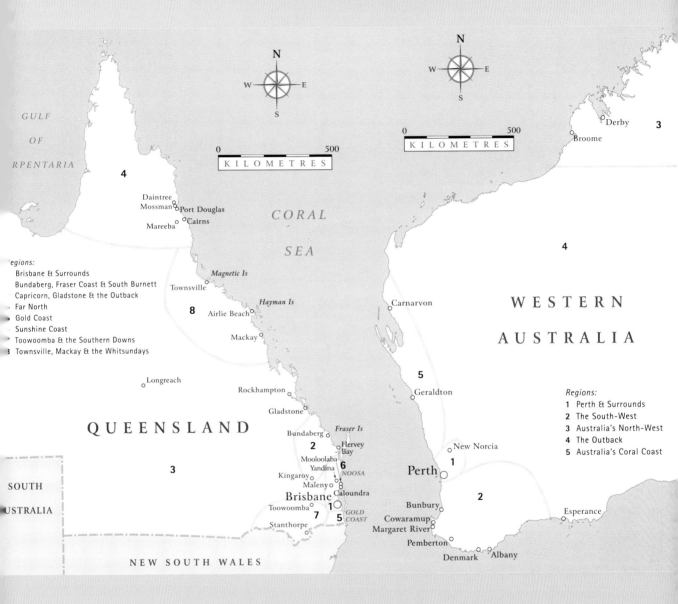

GULF

OF

CARPENTARIA

CORAL

SEA

Regions:
Brisbane & Surrounds
Bundaberg, Fraser Coast & South Burnett
Capricorn, Gladstone & the Outback
Far North
Gold Coast
Sunshine Coast
Toowoomba & the Southern Downs
Townsville, Mackay & the Whitsundays

4

Daintree
Mossman
Port Douglas
Cairns
Mareeba

8

Magnetic Is
Townsville

Hayman Is
Airlie Beach

Mackay

Longreach

Rockhampton
Gladstone

QUEENSLAND

3

Bundaberg
2
Hervey Bay
Fraser Is

Mooloolaba
Yandina
Kingaroy
Maleny
6
NOOSA
Caloundra

Brisbane
1
Toowoomba
7 **5**
GOLD COAST
Stanthorpe

SOUTH
AUSTRALIA

NEW SOUTH WALES

WESTERN

AUSTRALIA

Derby
Broome
3

4

Carnarvon

5
Geraldton

New Norcia
Perth
1

Bunbury
Cowaramup
Margaret River
Pemberton
Denmark Albany

2

Esperance

Regions:
1 Perth & Surrounds
2 The South-West
3 Australia's North-West
4 The Outback
5 Australia's Coral Coast

0   500
KILOMETRES

0   500
KILOMETRES

169

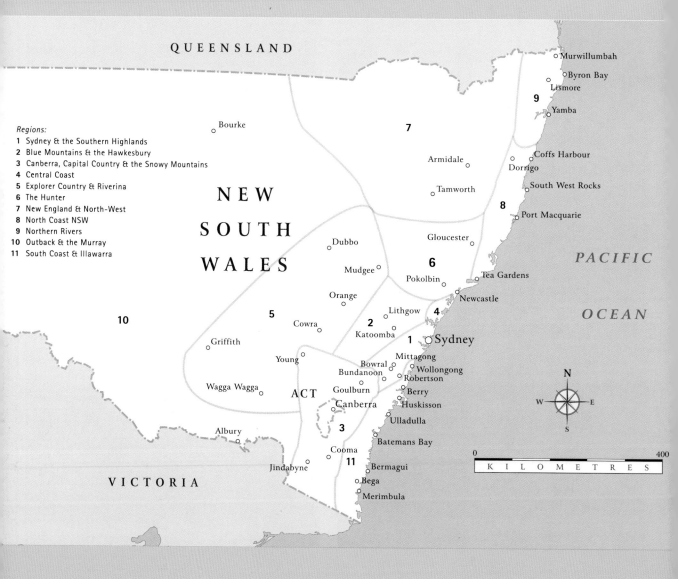

QUEENSLAND

Murwillumbah

Byron Bay

Lismore

9

Yamba

Bourke

Regions:
1 Sydney & the Southern Highlands
2 Blue Mountains & the Hawkesbury
3 Canberra, Capital Country & the Snowy Mountains
4 Central Coast
5 Explorer Country & Riverina
6 The Hunter
7 New England & North-West
8 North Coast NSW
9 Northern Rivers
10 Outback & the Murray
11 South Coast & Illawarra

7

Armidale

Coffs Harbour

Dorrigo

South West Rocks

Tamworth

8

Port Macquarie

NEW

SOUTH

WALES

Gloucester

Dubbo

Mudgee

6

Pokolbin

Tea Gardens

PACIFIC

Orange

Lithgow

4

Newcastle

5

Cowra

2

OCEAN

10

Griffith

Young

Katoomba

1

Sydney

Mittagong

Bowral

Wollongong

Bundanoon

Robertson

Wagga Wagga

ACT

Goulburn

Berry

Huskisson

N

Canberra

Ulladulla

W   E

Albury

3

Batemans Bay

S

Cooma

11

Bermagui

0   400

Jindabyne

Bega

VICTORIA

Merimbula

K I L O M E T R E S

VICTORIA

Mildura

Robinvale

Swan Hill

Regions:
1 Melbourne
2 Bays & Peninsulas
3 Goldfields
4 Goulburn Murray Waters
5 Lakes & Wilderness
6 Legends, Wine & High
Country

7 Macedon Ranges & Spa Country
8 Murray & the Outback
9 Phillip Island & Gippsland
10 The Grampians
11 The Great Ocean Road
12 Yarra Valley & the Dandenong Ranges

N
W E
S

Echuca

Shepparton

Wodonga
Rutherglen

Beechworth
Milawa
Bright

6

8

Bendigo

4

Halls Gap
10
Pomonal

3

Daylesford

Ballarat

7 Macedon
Coldstream

Healesville

12

5

Melbourne

2
Geelong

1
Dandenong

2
Sorrento

9

Lakes Entrance

11

Warrnambool

Port
Fairy

Port Campbell

Portsea

Phillip Is

Mornington
Peninsula

Apollo Bay

0

KILOMETR

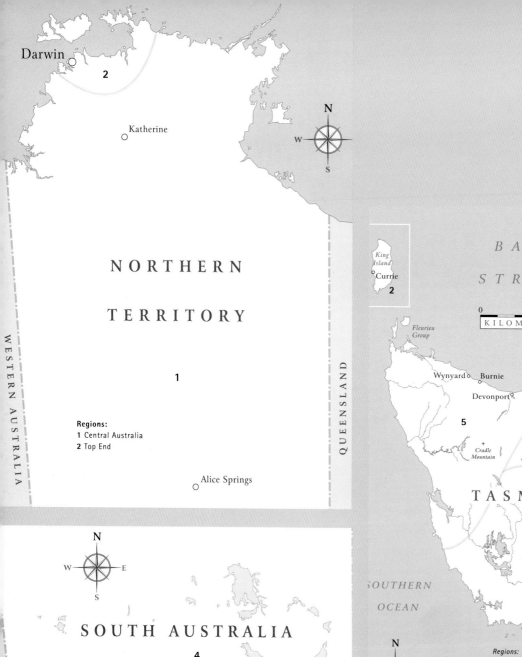
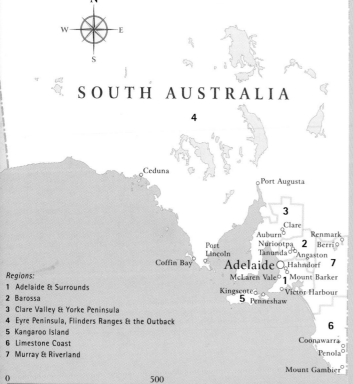
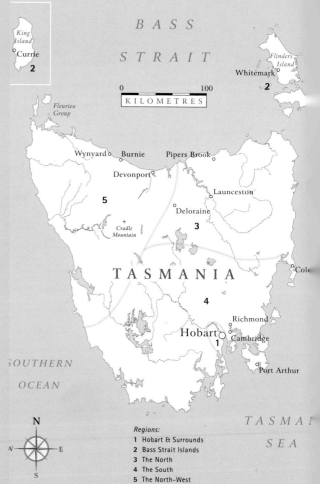

INDEX

aniseed myrtle, 72, 80
apples, Fine Apple Tart, 136
    Forest Grove Apple Cake, 157
    Hot Smoked Ocean Trout, Apple and Avocado
      Salad with Limoncello Dressing, 40
    Meredith Ewe's Milk Feta, Walnut and Apple
      Salad with Red Wine Dressing, 49
    Sisters Rock Apple Cake, 152
Artichokes with Basque Flavoured Salsa, 28
avocado
    Hot Smoked Ocean Trout, Apple and Avocado
      Salad with Limoncello Dressing, 40
    ice-cream, 119
    Not Chocolate Meringue, 125
banana
    Banana Tart Tatin with Rum and Raisin Ice-cream,
      119
    Raspberry and Banana Muffins, 155
beef
    Aged Black Angus Beef Tenderloin with Beef
      Cheek Jus, Leek and Potato Gratin, 82-3
    Char-grilled Beef with Goldenbelle Stack on
      Mesclun, 19
    Grilled Manning Valley Beef Fillet with Three
      Mustard Sauce and Garlic Potato Mash, 73
beetroot
    Beetroot and Feta Risotto, 29
    Grilled Beef Fillet with Three Mustard Sauce, Baby
      Beetroot and Snowpeas, 73
    Red on Red Salad, 52
    Souper Beet Soup, 57
Black Bean Vinaigrette, 101
blackcurrant
    Cheesecake Semifreddo, 134
    Garden Salad, 52
Black Forest Pie, 126
Black Sapote Torte, 124
blueberries
    Comboyne Blueberries Flambe with Marrook Farm
      Yoghurt Lime Mousse, 120
Bush Billy Tea, 98, 99, 100
cabbage
    Asian Red Cabbage Salad, 53
    Sesame Crusted Chicken with Asian Slaw and
      Chilli Coriander Dressing, 84
Capsicum, baked, with goat cheese, 36
cheese
    Baked Capsicum with Goat Cheese, 36
    Beetroot and Feta Risotto, 29
    Black Paddock Terrine of Salmon with Capers and
      Mascarpone, 32
    Buffalo Mozzarella with Eggplant Caponata, 27
    Bush Tea Veal with Mushrooms, Gorgonzola and
      Spirali Pasta, 98

Char-grilled Beef or Lamb and Goldenbelle Stack
    on Mesclun, 19
    Fetabelle Salsa, 112
    Fromagebelle and Spinach Cannelloni, 67
    Hazelnut Baked Borda White, 37
    Kenilworth Bruschetta, 26
    Kenilworth Marinated Feta, 160
    Kenilworth Ricotta Breakfast, 15
    Meredith Ewe's Milk Feta, Walnut and Apple
      Salad with Red Wine Dressing, 49
    Smoked Salmon with Kervella Goat Cheese in
      Bread Cases, 39
    Tart of Braised Wallaby Shanks with Onion and
      Goat Cheese Soufflé, 92-3
    Three Cheese Torta with Caramelised Onion and
      Roasted Pumpkin, 71
cheesecake
    Blackcurrent Semifreddo, 134
    Black Forest Pie, 126
    Lavender, 142
    Raspberry Liqueur Glaze, with, 135
    Quark Chocolate Flan, 129
cherry
    liqueur sauce, 14
    Smoked Chicken or Quail with Savoury Cherry
      Sauce, 90
    Spicy Plum, Cherry and Shiraz Relish, 162
chestnuts
    bread, 157
    Nesselrode Pudding, 127
    Nirvana Chestnut Ice-cream, 127
chicken
    Kelp Chicken Delight, 85
    Sesame Crusted Chicken with Asian Slaw and
      Chilli Coriander Dressing, 84
    Smoked Chicken or Quail with Savoury Cherry
      Sauce, 90
chickpeas
    Moroccan Spiced Chickpea and Roasted Pumpkin
      Soup, 61
chocolate
    Belgian Chocolate Bread, 153
    Chocolate, Date and Almond Torte, 145
    Mandarin, Almond and Chocolate (flourless) Cake,
      122
    Milk Chocolate and Tangerine Mousse, 140
    oil, 42
    Quark Chocolate Flan, 129
    Venison Carpaccio with Chocolate Oil and
      Hazelnut Crunch, 42
Cinnamon Stars (Zimmt sterne), 149
Citrus Twist tea
    cake, 154
    iced tea, 165
    Poached Salmon in Citrus Twist Broth with
      Sansho Pepper, 58
    Snapper Fillet with Citrus Twist Crust, 101
coconut milk
    Curried Zucchini and Sweet Potato Soup with

173

Coconut Milk, 59
Lemon Myrtle and Macadamia Green Seafood
   Curry, 72
coffee
   Sauce Arabica, 93
Creme anglaise, 123
Daiquiri, The World's Best, 165
dates
   Chocolate, Date and Almond Torte, 145
   Not Chocolate Meringue, 125
   Dorrigo pepper, 22, 72
duck
   Chinese Barbecued Duck Risotto, 76
   Roasted Soy Duck with Steamed Spiced Eggplant
      and Tatsoi Salad, 68-9
eggplant
   Buffalo Mozzarella with Eggplant Caponata, 27
   Honey Glazed Eggplant Talinga Grove, 36
   Roasted Soy Duck with Steamed Spiced Eggplant
      and Tatsoi Salad, 68-9
   Tian of Eggplant, 95
elderflower
   emulsion, 88
   Semifreddo and Apple Tisane, 132
fennel
   Char-grilled Yamba Prawns, Tomato, Fennel and
      Olive Braise, 75
   Peppered King Dory, 95
   Yarra Valley Salmon Rillettes with Pickled Fennel
      Salad, 31
figs
   chutney, 89
   Fig and Prosciutto Salad, 50
   Fig, Raisin and Chilli Relish, 161
   Jess's Fresh Fig Salad, 51
fish see also seafood
   Baby Salmon and Silver Beet, 86
   Barramundi in Paperbark with Fragrant Salsa, 80
   Barrington Perch Fillets Poached in Lemon Myrtle
      Macadamia Nut Coconut Sauce, 20
   Black Paddock Terrine of Salmon with Capers and
      Mascarpone, 32
   Crispy Skin Native Silver Perch, 64
   Fish Cakes with Mango and Lemon Myrtle
      Dressing, 22
   Gravlax and Caviar in Buttermilk Jelly, 21
   Hot Smoked Ocean Trout, Apple and Avocado
      Salad with Limoncello Dressing, 40
   Joe's Bush Billy Tea Swordfish with Marinated
      Zucchini and Tomato Glaze, 98
   Light Curry-spiced Coral Trout with Watermelon
      Salsa and Crispy Seaweed, 77
   Peppered King Dory, 95
   Poached Salmon in Citrus Twist Broth with
      Sansho Pepper, 58
   Rolled Atlantic Salmon with Du Puy Lentils and
      Ashbolt Elderflower Emulsion, 88-9
   Salad of Smoked Eel and Smoked Trout Sausage
      on a Potato Pancake, 34-5

   Smoked Salmon with Kervella Goat Cheese in
      Bread Cases, 39
   Snapper Fillet with Citrus Twist Crust, 101
   Tempura Nori Rolled Atlantic Salmon with Blue
      Swimmer Crab and Ginger Mousse, 70
   Tuna Trevalla Sashimi, 43
   Yarra Valley Salmon Rillettes with Pickled Fennel
      Salad, 31
Granita, fruit liqueur, 136
Gravlax and Caviar in Buttermilk Jelly, 21
hazelnuts
   Baked Borda White, 37
   Souper Beet Soup, 57
   Venison Carpaccio with Chocolate Oil and
      Hazelnut Crunch, 42
   Warm Salad, 48
hemp
   butter, 125
   nut, 125
   oil, 57
honey
   Honey and Lavender Cream Dessert, 130
   Vanilla Bean Panna Cotta with Honey Tuiles, 139-
      40
ice-cream
   avocado, 119
   Banana Tart Tatin with Rum and Raisin, 119
   Nirvana Chestnut, 127
   'Simply' Delicate, 142
juniper berries, 94, 104
kangaroo
   Seared, with Pepperberry Sauce and Warrigal
      Greens, 102
   see also wallaby
Kangaroo Island cranberries, 37
lamb
   Braised Lamb Shanks with Quinces, Pomegranate
      and Cinnamon, 94
   Cowra Lamb Rump with Spicy Du Puy Lentils and
      Roast Pumpkin, 65
   Davidson Plum Lamb with Bush Spices, 72
   Joe's Bush Billy Tea Lamb with Roesti Potatoes
      and Spinach, 98
lavender, 130
   cheesecake, 142
   fruitcake, 155
   Honey and Lavender Cream Dessert, 130
   Lemon and Lavender Shortbread Talinga Grove,
      148
lemon
   biscotti, 148
   Citrus Twist Cake, 154
   Citrus Twist Iced Tea, 165
   Lemon and Lavender Shortbread Talinga Grove,
      148
Lemongrass and Palm Sugar Panna Cotta with
   Orange and Chilli Caramel, 137
lemon myrtle
   Barramundi in Paperbark with Fragrant Salsa, 80

Barrington Perch Fillets Poached in Lemon Myrtle
  Macadamia Nut Coconut Sauce, 20
cheesecake, 117, 121
Davidson Plum Lamb with Bush Spices, 72
Fish Cakes with Mango and Lemon Myrtle
  Dressing, 22
Lemon Myrtle and Macadamia Green Seafood
  Curry, 72
Sauteed Prawns and Scallops with Lemon Myrtle,
  22
slice, 121
Tempura Gulf Bugs on Lemongrass Skewers with
  Sweet Lemon Myrtle Dipping Sauce, 78
lentils
  Cowra Lamb Rump with Spicy Du Puy Lentils and
    Roast Oumpkin, 65
  Rolled Atlantic Salmon with Du Puy Lentils, 88-9
lime
  Comboyne Blueberries Flambe with Marrook Farm
    Yoghurt Lime Mousse, 120
  Crispy Wonton Prawns with Red Pawpaw Salsa,
    Lime and Tomato Chutney, 24
  Steamed Sydney Rock Oysters with Kaffir Lime,
    Chilli, Ginger and Tamari, 23
  The World's Best Daiquiri, 165
macadamia nuts
  Barramundi in Paperbark with Fragrant Salsa, 80
  Barrington Perch Fillets Poached in Lemon Myrtle
    Macadamia Nut Coconut Sauce, 20
  Lemon Myrtle and Macadamia Green Seafood
    Curry, 72
  Rolled Atlantic Salmon with Du Puy Lentils, 88-9
  Souper Beet Soup, 57
Mandarin, Almond and Chocolate (flourless) Cake,
  122
mango
  Fish Cakes with Mango and Lemon Myrtle
    Dressing, 22
Mohnkloese, 131
Mountain pepperberries, 102
mushrooms
  Blue Swimmer Crab and Ginger Mousse, 70
  Bush Tea Veal with Mushrooms, Gorgonzola and
    Spirali Pasta, 98
  Mushroom and Pea Lasagne, 87
  Seared Scallops with Double Mushroom Custard
    and Roasted Black Mushrooms, 44-5
  Simple Nibble Mushrooms, 30
olives
  Black Olive and Thyme Tart with Olive Oil Pastry,
    38
  Braised Rabbit Gnocchi with Tomatoes, Chorizo,
    Rosemary and Olives, 96
  Char-grilled Yamba Prawns, Tomato, Fennel and
    Olive Braise, 75
  Tapenade, 160, 163
Orange and Chilli Caramel, Candied Chillies and
  Orange Zest, 137
pancakes

Hotcakes with Cherry Liqueur Sauce, 14
Salad of Smoked Eel and Smoked Trout Sausage
  on a Potato Pancake, 34-5
pasta
  Braised Rabbit Gnocchi with Tomatoes, Chorizo,
    Tosemary and Olives, 96
  Bush Tea Veal with Mushrooms, Gorgonzola and
    Spirali Pasta, 98
  Fromagebelle and Spinach Cannelloni, 67
  Mushroom and Pea Lasagne, 87
  Pappardelle Pasta with Blue Swimmer Crab,
    Lilliput Capers, Salsa Verde and Roma Tomato, 108
pawpaw (also papaya)
  Crispy Wonton Prawns with Red Pawpaw Salsa,
    Lime and Tomato Chutney, 24
  Tempura Gulf Bugs on Lemongrass Skewers with
    Green Papaya Salad, 78
Pear Pudding, 128
Pheasant
  Crispy Skinned Pheasant Breast with Toasted
    Barley Risotto and Roast Carrot Sauce, 104
pineapple
  Chilli Jam, 79
  Stir Fry Pork with Pineapple, Ginger and Yellow
    Bean Sauce, 81
plums
  Davidson Plum Lamb with Bush Spices, 72
  Spicy Plum, Cherry and Shiraz Relish, 162
pomegranate, 94
Poppy Seed Clumps (Mohnkloese), 131
pork
  Macedon Ranges Regional Rabbit and Pork
    Cassoulet, 106-7
  Rillettes, 43
  Stir Fry Pork with Pineapple, Ginger and Yellow
    Bean Sauce, 81
  Twice Cooked Mareeba Pork Shoulder with Spring
    Onion Rice Cake, 79
possum
  Sweet Spiced Possum Braise, 90
potato
  Garlic Potato Mash, 73
  Gratin, 83
  Joe's Bush Billy Tea Lamb with Roesti Potatoes
    and Spinach, 98
  Pan-fried Gnocchi, 97
  Salad of Smoked Eel and Smoked Trout Sausage
    on a Potato Pancake, 34-5
  'Simple' Oven Baked Potatoes, 113
  'Simple' Squashed Potatoes, 112
Prosciutto, 50
prawns see seafood
pumpkin
  Cowra Lamb Rump with Spicy Du Puy Lentils and
    Roast Pumpkin, 65
  Moroccan Spiced Chickpea and Roasted Pumpkin
    Soup, 61
  'Simple' Surprise Pumpkin, 113
  Three Cheese Torta with Caramelised Onion and

Roasted Pumpkin, 71
Quail
    eggs, 64
    Smoked Quail with Savoury Cherry Sauce, 90
    Tian of Eggplant, 95
quince
    Braised Lamb Shanks with Quinces,
      Pomegranate and Cinnamon, 94
    cake, 116
rabbit
    Braised Rabbit Gnocchi with Tomatoes,
      Chorizo, Rosemary and Olives, 96-7
    Macedon Ranges Regional Rabbit and Pork
      Cassoulet, 106-7
raspberries
    Black Forest Pie, 126
    Cheesecake with Raspberry Liqueur Glaze
    Raspberry and Banana Muffins, 155
    Yoghurt Dessert, 144
rhubarb
    Rhubarb and Semillon Relish, 161
    Strawberry-rhubarb Under Meringue Gratin,
      123
rice
    Beetroot and Feta Risotto, 29
    Chinese Barbecued Duck Risotto, 76
    Toasted Barley Risotto, 105
Rosewater syrup, 138
seafood see also fish
    Char-grilled Yamba Prawns, Tomato, Fennel
      and Olive Braise with Saffron Mayonnaise,
      75
    Crispy Wonton Prawns with Red Pawpaw
      Salsa, Lime and Tomato Chutney, 24
    Gravlax and Caviar in Buttermilk Jelly, 21
    Lemon Myrtle and Macadamia Green Seafood
      Curry, 72
    Pappardelle Pasta with Blue Swimmer Crab,
      Lilliput Capers, Salsa Verde and Roma Tomato,
      108
    Prawn Bisque, 56
    Salad of Smoked Eel and Smoked Trout
      Sausage on a Potato Pancake, 34-5
    Sauteed Prawns and Scallops with Lemon
      Myrtle, 22
    Seared Scallops with Double Mushroom
      Custard, and Tomato Beurre Blanc, 44-5
    Steamed Sydney Rock Oysters with Kaffir
      Lime, Chilli, Ginger and Tamari, 23
    Tempura Gulf Bugs on Lemongrass Skewers
      with Green Papaya Salad, 78
    Tempura Nori Rolled Atlantic Salmon with
      Blue Swimmer Crab and Ginger Mousse, 70
seaweed, 77, 85
Smoking, method, 33
Spinach and Fromagebelle Cannelloni, 67
strawberries
    Black Forest Pie, 126
    Strawberry-rhubarb Under Meringue Gratin,

    123
sweet potato
    Curried Zucchini and Sweet Potato Soup with
      Coconut Milk, 59
    mash, 93
Tamarillos, poached, 124
tomato
    Braised Rabbit Gnocchi with Tomatoes, Chori-
      zo, Rosemary and Olives, 96
    Char-grilled Yamba Prawns, Tomato, Fennel
      and Olive Braise, 75
    Fetabelle Salsa, 112
    Joe's Bush Billy Tea Swordfish with
      Marinated Zucchini and Tomato Glaze, 98
    Pappardelle Pasta with Blue Swimmer Crab,
      Lilliput Capers, Salsa Verde and Roma Tomato,
      108
    Seared Scallops with Double Mushroom
      Custard, and Tomato Beurre Blanc, 44-5
    Simple Oven Baked Potatoes, 113
    Simple Squashed Potatoes, 112
    Simple Surprise Pumpkin, 113
    Simply Delicate Ice-cream, 142
    Simply Green Tomato Dip or Spread, 30
    Stuffed Vine Leaves, 18
Taro chips, 78
Tazziberries, 132
veal
    Bush Tea Veal with Mushrooms, Gorgonzola
      and Spirali Pasta, 98
venison
    Carpaccio with Chocolate Oil and Hazelnut
      Crunch, 42
    Sichuan Pepper and Soy Cured Venison and
      Chinese Red Date Salad, 66
Vanilla Bean Panna Cotta with Berries in
    Rosewater Syrup, 138
Vine leaves, stuffed, 18
Wallaby
    Tart of Braised Wallaby Shanks with Onion
      and Goat Cheese Soufflé, 92-3
    Stir Fry, 91
walnuts
    Marsala walnuts, 51
    Meredith Ewe's Milk Feta, Walnut and Apple
      Salad with Red Wine Dressing, 49
    Spanish Walnut Cake, 156
Warrigal greens, 48, 102
watermelon, Salsa, 77
zucchini
    Curried Zucchini and Sweet Potato Soup with
      Coconut Milk, 59
    Joe's Bush Billy Tea Swordfish with
      Marinated Zucchini and Tomato Glaze, 98